Straddling the Border

Straddling

IMMIGRATION POLICY AND THE INS

the Border

Lisa Magaña

UNIVERSITY OF TEXAS PRESS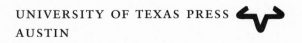
AUSTIN

FIGURE SOURCES

Figure 1: Author's chart.

Figures 2, 3: From data provided by Diane Weaver, INS Director of Equal Opportunity, April 2000.

Figures 4, 5, 6: From "Breakdown by PATCOB Code,: provided by Diane Weaver, INS Director of Equal Opportunity, October 2000.

Figure 7: From "Immigration and Naturalization Service Age Breakdown within Pay Plan," provided by Diane Weaver, INS Director of Equal Opportunity, October 2000.

Figure 8: From "Breakdown by PATCOB Code," provided by Diane Weaver, INS Director of Equal Opportunity, October 2000.

Figure 9: From "Immigration and Naturalization Service Average Salary Breakdown for PATCOB," provided by Diane Weaver, INS Director of Equal Opportunity, October 2000.

Figures 10–17: From INS Statistical Yearbook, 1998.

LIBRARY OF CONGRESS CATALOGING-IN-PUBLICATION DATA

Magaña, Lisa.
    Straddling the border : immigration policy and the INS / by Lisa Magaña. — 1st ed.
        p.   cm.
Includes bibliographical references and index.
    ISBN 0-292-70521-2 (alk. paper) — ISBN 0-292-70176-4 (pbk. : alk. paper)
    1. United States—Emigration and immigration—Government policy.
2. United States.   Immigration and Naturalization Service.   I. Title.
JV6483 .M27   2003
325.73—dc22

                                                                    2003016074

For
Robert and Isabella

Contents

Figures

Tables

Acknowledgments

I want to thank in particular two friends and colleagues, Ed Escobar and Cecilia Menjivar, who generously offered important suggestions for improving the manuscript. I am grateful to the anonymous reviewers of the manuscript for their meticulous comments and recommendations. I would also like to thank my colleagues in the Chicana/o Studies Department at Arizona State University, Vicki Ruiz, Cordelia Candelaria, Vera Galaviz, and Arturo Aldama, who gave me time, encouragement, and resources to finish this project. My research assistants, Mike Rizzo, Mathew Martinez, and Flavio Alberino, also provided important help. I thank Harry Pachon, Jose Calderon, Dan Mazmanian, and Andrew Murphy for their guidance.

On a personal note, I want to thank my family, Dora, Gracie, Sharilyn, Cindy, and Turo. My gratitude also goes out to my dear friends and extended family, Shirline, Ron, and Jan for their always positive assistance.

Straddling the Border

Chapter One

The Immigration Policy Process

A RECURRING THEME

IN 1999 I ATTENDED A MEETING with Doris Meissner, federal commissioner of the Immigration and Naturalization Service (INS). The purpose of the meeting was to discuss the mounting immigration crisis in Arizona. The number of immigrant deaths in the desert had quadrupled since 1993. An increase in the number of Border Patrol agents in Texas and California had resulted in undocumented immigrants attempting to enter the United States through the less guarded Nogales-Arizona region, where temperatures can reach a staggering 120 degrees. Unfortunately, fewer Border Patrol agents results in less assistance for immigrants unprepared for the brutal Arizona climate.

Before this meeting, I talked to two high-ranking INS officials. I told them that I was a political scientist conducting research on undocumented Mexican immigration.[1] They informed me that there are two issues that need examination in immigration research. First, the public generally does not understand what the agency does. One INS representative remarked, "People only see Border Patrol agents. What we really do is a lot of paperwork. Someone needs to do research on the bureaucrats, but I guess that is not sexy enough." Although substantial resources and manpower are directed to enforcement policies, such as patrolling the border, it is the bureaucrats who process and have significant influence on Mexican immigrants. Second, many of the policies assigned to the agency in the past two decades are not based on realistic approaches to curbing immigration. Rather, immigration policies are motivated by the political and popular sentiments of the moment.

After this discussion, I reviewed the research on the agency. My investigation confirmed what the INS officials had told me. Indeed, I found that there are few studies on the bureaucrats of the agency or on the effect that immigration policies have on the INS. The purpose of this book is to bridge this gap. I show how major immigration policies in the past twenty years have influenced INS bureaucrats and the quality of service afforded to Mexican immigrants. How immigration polices are crafted and then implemented by the INS is what I define as the "immigration policy process."

The way in which an agency carries out policy mandates has a great deal to do with whether those policies will be successes or failures. That is, from a theoretical research perspective, organizational characteristics such as (1) impossible and multiple tasks, (2) illogical and shifting federal mandates, and (3) apparent ineffectiveness and inefficiency merit consideration. This book also explores how the INS implements immigration policies despite what appear to be illogical organizational mandates. It shows how policies and agency directives are based on the prevailing political economy, with little consideration of the efficiency of these policies or the effect on the target group, in this case, Mexican immigrants. In many ways, this book is also about policy congruence, that is, making the policies fit with the design and abilities of the agency.

According to the INS *1998 Statistical Yearbook* (1999), Mexican immigrants are the largest group admitted into the United States legally, as well as the largest group naturalized. Mexican immigrants are also the largest group apprehended and deported by the INS. Clearly, the role of the INS in the lives of Mexican immigrants must be considered in immigration debates as well as in policy reform.

Popular Sentiment

Immigration issues historically have been clouded by emotion, especially during the past twenty years. According to a national Gallup Poll conducted in 1993, Americans believe that most immigrants are undocumented. Americans also believe that most undocumented immigrants are Latin American, typically Mexican, and that they take more than they contribute to the U.S. economy (De Sipio and de la Garza 1998).

Espenshade and Balanger (1998) examined American attitudes toward different types of immigrants based on their ethnicity. They found that Mexican immigrants were ranked lowest and European immigrants were ranked highest in positive social attributes, such as family values and working hard. Mexican immigrants were perceived as more likely to use welfare and commit more crime. Furthermore, Americans believe that the United States is admitting too many immigrants from Asia and Latin America. These data clearly reflect Americans' passionate interest in "illegal" immigration over "legal" immigration. This is further evidenced by the fact that nine out of ten respondents thought the United States should do a better job of enforcing its borders. Interestingly, these researchers established a clear link between public attitudes toward immigration issues and economic conditions. They wrote that attitudes toward immigration "are partially conditioned by the state of the macroeconomy and that these attitudes harden when employment prospects for workers dim" (Espenshade and Balanger 1998: 367).

Political Agenda Setting

Short and Magaña (1998) found that undocumented immigration,[2] as a political agenda, was a significant issue in elections during the 1990s. Politicians are aware of immigration reform's value as an election year issue. Between 1992 and 1998, for example, there were a number of political referenda and initiatives designed to reduce undocumented immigration at both the state and national levels, particularly during the congressional and presidential election cycles of 1996. We also found that after elections, the number of such proposals decreased dramatically (see Tables 1, 2, 3).

Tables 1, 2, and 3 show that immigration, as a political issue, was championed by Republicans and that Mexican immigrants were constructed negatively in terms of their influence on the economy and cultural norms.

Politicians shape immigration issues to their advantage, to move other political agendas to the forefront. An INS representative once told me, "Congress treats immigration law as something less important than tax or drug or other laws. Furthermore, members of Congress criticize the INS for its inability to control immigration without really understanding what we do" (pers. com. 1999).

It is important to note that there are no clearly defined ideological or partisan agendas surrounding undocumented immigration. Although the past twenty years show that in general Republicans are more likely than Democrats to advocate restricting immigration, some conservative Republicans extol the virtues of hardworking immigrants as good for the economy, and some liberal Democrats decry the presence of undocumented immigrants because they negatively affect the environment or cause a decrease in wages. This lack of clarity on the part of politicians and political parties tends to make the issue of undocumented immigration reform less clear to constituents, as both ends of the political spectrum base their arguments on populist and emotional appeals. The result has been policies based on emotional appeal with little concern for the agency's capacity to carry out its assigned duties.

Table 1. *Frequency of articles referencing Mexican immigration by political affiliation*

Political Party	Frequency of Newspaper Articles	
	N	PERCENT
Republican	253	61
Republican and Democrat	100	24.1
Democrat	40	9.6
Other	4	1
No party reference	18	4.3

Note: N = 415 newspaper articles during 1992–1998.

Table 2. *Frequency of articles referencing Mexican immigration by political level*

Political Party	Frequency of Newspaper Articles	
	N	PERCENT
Federal	235	56.6
State	116	28
Local	45	10.8
Combination	19	4.6

Note: N = 415 newspaper articles during 1992–1998.

Table 3. *Frequency of articles referencing Mexican immigration by themes, both positive and negative*

| | Frequency of Newspaper Articles | | | |
| | Positive | | Negative | |
THEME	N	PERCENT	N	PERCENT
Combination of themes mentioned	83	20.0	301	72.5
Voter issues	65	15.7	35	8.4
Economic	2	0.5	19	4.6
Cultural	1	0.2	11	2.7
No negative references	264	63.6	46	11.1

Note: N = 415 for each valence (positive and negative).

Political party affiliation is based on a variety of factors. First, if there is significant representation of elected officials of one party in the community where one resides, then there is greater likelihood one will choose that party. Second, a person may choose one party over the other because of its stance on social and ethical issues, such as government spending, the death sentence, or abortion. Third, a person may choose to remain aligned with the party with which his or her parents are affiliated. Because people are not likely to change party affiliation, voter registration drives in Latino communities are crucial in recruiting and sustaining membership. Given these factors, Mexican Americans generally identify themselves as Democrats.

Historically, the role of the federal government has also solidified party preference among Latinos. President Franklin D. Roosevelt's New Deal, for instance, implemented policies—housing, urban development, and employment programs—that assisted Mexican Americans and brought them into the Democratic Party. And during the 1960s, President Lyndon Johnson's Great Society implemented public works, medical assistance, and job training programs that also solidified the relationship between Mexican Americans and the Democratic Party. Another pivotal event that strengthened the union between Mexican Americans and the Democratic Party was the "Viva Kennedy Campaign."

Recently, Mexican Americans have shifted slightly their party preference. For some, the Republican agenda on issues such as family values and abortion has been more meaningful. Because Mexican Americans constitute the largest and fastest growing Latino group in the United States and no longer vote monolithically, they have become a crucial swing vote in political campaigns.

Political parties are aware of the potential voting power of Mexican Americans and are actively courting them for the first time in history. Exit polls indicate that they are voting in greater numbers than ever before. Their presence in states such as Texas, California, and Florida can mean the difference between winning or losing elections. The Democratic Party has taken a more favorable stance on immigration, although more recently Republicans have begun to use immigration as a means of courting voters as well.

Immigrant Misperceptions

Politicians and candidates may disingenuously use pejorative social stereotypes when discussing immigrants in order to appeal to their constituents' fears. For example, when Pete Wilson ran for the presidency in 1996 he maintained that hundreds of thousands of immigrants come to the United States to take advantage of social welfare. In a campaign speech delivered in front of the Statue of Liberty, Wilson said, "The illegal immigrants are coming, and that means crime, more welfare mothers and lotsa spicy food!" (*Boston Globe*, September 1, 1995). This is simply untrue, as social welfare is not allocated to individuals in the United States who are undocumented. Congress bars undocumented immigrants from receiving Aid for Families with Dependent Children (AFDC), Supplemental Security Income (SSI), Food Stamps, Medicaid (except in emergencies), housing assistance, legal services, unemployment insurance, and student financial aid. Some studies have found that Mexican immigrants are even less likely to use available welfare resources than other groups because they are more likely to use home remedies, are unfamiliar with available resources, and are fearful of deportation (e.g., de la Torre and Estrada 2001).

Although rates of use are difficult to measure, studies consistently indicate that social services are not a significant magnet for undocumented immigrants. Simply put, immigrants migrate for employment. Politicians' willingness to use immigration issues to gain election and the ease with which they are able to sway voters reflect a general misunderstanding by the public regarding immigration issues and social services. Other misunderstandings include the actual number of undocumented immigrants, their reasons for migrating, and our economic dependence on this population.

Immigrants are a highly diverse group, some of them with legal status and some of them with undocumented status. Some immigrants, both legal and illegal, are well educated, and some provide investment and business opportunities in their communities. According to the 2000 census, approximately 10 percent of the total U.S. population is foreign born. Mexican legal immigrants make up approximately 30 percent of this immigrant population.

Figures for undocumented immigrants are never precise. Nevertheless, the best estimates put the total undocumented immigrant population at approximately 2 percent to 3 percent of the U.S. population, with approximately half coming from Mexico. The majority of the undocumented population comprises persons who entered the United States legally for business or pleasure and who then failed to leave after their visas expired (INS 1999). Undocumented immigrants who enter the United States at areas other than border points of entry are referred to as entries without inspections (EWIs).

Reasons for migrating to the United States are complex. A voluminous body of literature suggests that people migrate for a number of reasons (Massey et al. 1987; Portes and Rumbaut 1996; Menjivar 2000) including a lack of employment opportunities in the sending country (Sassen 1994) and employment demands for cheap labor in the receiving country (Cornelius 1998), among other reasons. Further, immigration, particularly Mexican immigration, is the result of economic expansion policies facilitated by the United States. U.S. border states and Mexico are interconnected more than ever as a result of trade and liberalization policies. For instance, attempts to enhance economic expansion, such as the North American Free Trade Agreement (NAFTA), have had the effect of leaving millions of Mexicans out of the restructuring who then see the need to migrate (Chapa 1998).

Social and Economic Impacts

The social and economic impacts of demographic shifts may be surprising to the general public. For instance, studies show that the mere presence of immigrants in the economy results in a net gain in tax revenue, both federal and local, as well as overall spending in consumption (e.g., Fix and Passel 1994). Immigrant presence also creates jobs for American workers and does not seem to cause a rise in unemployment (Briggs and Moore 1994). However, foreign workers are susceptible to wage and employment exploitation, they are imported and repatriated in times of high unemployment, and they serve as scapegoats during economic crises (Wilson 1997).

Organizational Studies

The INS is responsible for enforcing immigration laws and servicing immigrants (Morris 1985). Researchers have found that this dual mission of the agency influences its representatives' ability to carry out immigration policies. The contradictory goals of policy objectives, both formal and informal, "serve to weaken the commitment on the part of INS representatives to implement organizational directives" (Calavita 1992: 9). Although the agency's enforcement activities generate a significant amount of attention, they are only one part of its overall mission. One study has shown that the public's tendency to believe that the INS is more interested in enforcement than in service deters legal Mexican immigrants from going to the agency, for example, to apply for naturalization (NALEO 1989).

In the past decade, a number of new immigration policies have been enacted. This has meant increased responsibilities and new roles and procedures for the agency to pursue. For instance, when President Bill Clinton mandated that immigrants be processed more expeditiously, INS representatives maintained that they were not given enough resources to do so. These mandates have not coincided with sufficient time to formulate clear agency guidelines, and as a result, implementation has suffered (Dunn 1996).

The environments in which policy actors operate have a great deal to do with the way policy decisions are made. Theorists find that environments inculcate systems of rewards and values in the minds of policy actors. For example, local policy actors who work in federal agencies have overwhelming and complex duties to perform. The expectations placed on them are ambiguous, vague, and often conflicting. Furthermore, since agencies are often large, actors can only see problems narrowly and independently of their connections to other issues. Therefore, agencies as a whole find it difficult to change or improve (Bardach and Kagan 1982; Kanter 1983).

Ripley (1986) explains that bureaucracies have the most pervasive influence on the implementation of policies. The factors that influence implementation are reorganization of staff and programs, available resources, and relationships with other agencies, clients, Congress, the president, and the institutional culture (Ripley 1986: 59). A variety of studies focusing on the INS's organizational constraints show that the agency must carry out immigration policies with inadequate funding (e.g., North and Portz 1989). One study shows that the agency's inability to carry out policies effectively was a result of poor organization and its management style (GAO 1991).

INS bureaucrats, particularly those at the local level, have the most influence over policy decisions. That is to say, regardless of the political and financial capital dedicated to a given immigration policy and the clarity with which it is defined, its effectiveness ultimately rests with the individual responsible for its implementation (Lipsky 1980; Romzek 1999). Therefore, the working conditions and the constraints placed on bureaucrats should be taken into consideration when assessing why policies succeed or fail. Because expectations placed on INS representatives tend to be ambiguous and their performance is difficult to measure, researchers have found that it is necessary to look at the policy process (Middleton 1997; Lindenberg 2000).

The Immigration Policy Process

What is missing from the research is the effect of the immigration policy process on the INS. Simply defined, the policy process refers to how policies are created and assigned to the agency and then how the agency carries out these policies. Consider the following theoretical framework as an illustration of the policy process for the INS.

Popular and emotional reactions to undocumented immigration develop at the local and state levels. When these sentiments eventually reach politicians at the federal level, Congress responds with new policy, which only creates more responsibilities for the INS. When these immigration policies are eventually assigned to the INS without appropriate improvements in the budget and the organizational infrastructure, the overall morale and quality of service suffers. The agency appears inefficient, and new policies are created to improve agency performance. (See Figure 1.)

Other federal agencies suffer from similar organizational problems. For example, the Food and Drug Administration is criticized for approving drugs either too slowly or too quickly. The Internal Revenue Service is responsible for collecting taxes but also for servicing the needs of clients. The Environmental Protection Agency must police industries and at the same time provide assistance. As a result of having a dual mission, procedures for resolving problems are complex and further complicated by external forces, such as popular sentiment and political grandstanding. Dual mission agencies are then criticized for their inability to process policy mandates.

Methodological Considerations

To study the immigration policy process and the INS, I used both quantitative and qualitative sources. Studies that examine the INS often use macro evaluations or quantitative approaches, such as assessing the rate of Border Patrol apprehensions, the number of people processed, or the amount of funding for operations in a given year. While these data are useful, I contend that they reflect only part of the picture for the reasons cited above. Therefore, this study relies on qualitative research methodologies as a means to supplement and enhance existing quantitative approaches. In particular, I conducted extensive interviews, which provide insight into

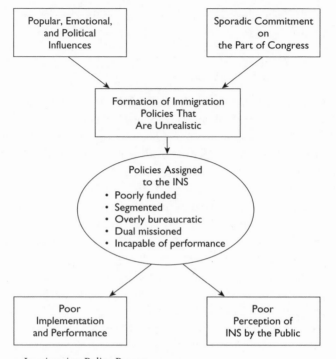

1. Immigration Policy Process

the organizational dynamics of the INS that traditional quantitative approaches are unable to describe fully. The interview process provides a unique perspective on the inner workings of the agency that are only partially reflected by other means such as survey research.

My methodology can be described as a field study approach, using in-depth interviews. This type of evaluation is based on the assumption that researchers at the local level are able to tap and interpret relevant policy developments and impacts. Field studies are useful when conducting research on the various levels of policy analysis, particularly during the implementation phase. Furthermore, in-depth interviews make it possible for researchers to clarify issues not articulated in immigration studies. For instance, they provide large amounts of information because they hold a respondent's attention longer than does a survey or telephone questionnaire. Respondents may also assist the researcher in pursuing areas not initially considered.

There are several problems associated with using in-depth interviews as a research tool, however. The respondent's comments cannot be generalized for the population at large, and the interviewer can have undue influence on the recorded responses. For instance, in-person interviews can produce highly biased data because of the interview process itself. "Recorded responses may reflect real-world facts or attitudes less than they reflect the reactions of respondents to a given interview, the biases of the interviewer, the liberties the interviewer takes in asking questions, or the interview style employed" (Manheim and Rich 1981: 118). It must be borne in mind, therefore, that a respondent's comments cannot be generalized to all agency employees.

From the mid-1990s to 2001, I conducted approximately eighty-five in-depth interviews with past and current federal commissioners of the INS, regional commissioners of the INS, and district directors and local INS representatives; sixty-three interviews were ultimately used for this book. Usually, the interviews lasted two to three hours. Some respondents were reinterviewed.

To gain access to some of the representatives in the agency, I had to submit to the public relations person and the district director of Los Angeles written statements describing why I wanted to interview INS individuals, my interview questions, the point of my research, and who would read these findings. After six weeks of correspondence and several in-person visits, I was authorized to interview representatives currently employed by the INS. After I interviewed some INS representatives it became much easier to interview others, as interviewees made calls or introduced me to other key respondents. The individuals I interviewed who were no longer employed by the INS provided candid insights into the agency's organizational environment. From the federal down to the street level, my sample responses represent the experiences of INS employees.

I also interviewed representatives of immigrant advocacy groups in order to understand some of the relevant constitutional and civil issues. Interviews were conducted in Los Angeles, California, Phoenix, Arizona, Santa Ana, California, and Washington, D.C. Like most of the INS respondents, most immigrant advocates wished to remain anonymous. Those respondents whose names appear in this book gave me permission. The list of interview questions can be found in Appendix 6. Table 4 provides information on the number of respondents by title.

Policy evaluations conducted by governmental agencies such as the Justice Department, the General Accounting Office (GAO), and the INS have been used. These agencies assess the performance of the INS at the federal, regional, and local levels. Surveys of immigrants who have dealt with the INS are also included, as are newspaper articles and other sources. Books,

Table 4. *Title and number of respondents*

Federal Commissioners of the INS	2
District Directors and Assistant Directors	5
Regional and Assistant Commissioners	7
INS Investigators and Staff	37
Immigrant Advocates	12

Note: Titles were consolidated. These respondents represent INS representatives who deal with immigration issues at the federal and state levels and on a day-to-day basis.

journals, and policy and immigration studies have also been used for this study.

Organization of This Book

This book is organized as follows. Chapter 2 reviews the history of U.S. immigration policy and demonstrates how the immigration policy process has evolved over the past one hundred fifty years.

Chapter 3 explores the organizational characteristics of the INS, its complexity, its highly bureaucratic nature, and its dual mission. The two main units within the INS—Enforcement and Service—have opposing objectives, which has led to serious organizational conflicts. In short, the agency is at odds with itself.

Chapter 4 examines how the INS has implemented the Immigration Reform and Control Act (IRCA), perhaps the most important immigration policy reform of the twentieth century. The overall objective of IRCA was to decrease the number of undocumented immigrants in the United States by implementing two provisions: employer sanctions and legalization. I demonstrate that while the INS is better known for implementing its enforcement directives, it is highly effective at implementing the legalization, or service, provision of IRCA.

Chapter 5 explores the recent impact of welfare reform on the INS. I show that with the passage of Proposition 187 in California and the 1996 Welfare Reform Act, the number of immigrants seeking naturalization tripled. INS representatives were unprepared for the significant increase in the number of immigrants applying for assistance.

In Chapter 6 I review my overall findings and make recommendations for improving agency performance. I also explore policy and research implications for future immigration policies.

Chapter Two | *Immigration Policies and Their Impact on the* INS

IN AN ATTEMPT TO ENABLE the INS to perform its newly assigned duties, it has been restructured and placed under various federal departments, Treasury, Labor, and Justice.[1] Based on the public and political climate, often dictated by racism, economic gains, competition for jobs, and even political opportunism, Congress responds with new policy, creating more responsibilities for the INS. As a result, Mexican immigrant presence has been pushed out of the country and pulled back in based on popular and political sentiment.

Immigration policies change quickly and considerably over time. Policy actors are left uncertain as to their goals and mandates, which results in poor policy implementation and the appearance of inadequacy.

History of Immigration Policy and the Shaping of the INS

There is no mention of restricting immigration in the Constitution; it provides only that Congress be responsible for immigration laws, that immigration is a federal issue, and that a fee be imposed on individuals entering the country. Concerns regarding immigration were minimal during the first one hundred years of statehood because the United States was a frontier society with ample employment for new arrivals. No major legislation regarding an immigration agency was passed and no official records were kept on immigration until the late 1800s.[2] (See Appendix 7 for a listing of all legislation having to do with immigration.)

In 1798 the Alien and Sedition Acts were passed. These laws were not created to control immigration but rather to control which individuals could become U.S. citizens. In the 1790s the political party in power, the Federalists, believed that immigrants from Europe would be more loyal to the opposing party, the Democratic Republicans. In an attempt to maintain their power, the Federalists lengthened the residence for naturalization to fourteen years. In 1802 these acts were repealed.

In the 1850s an anti-immigrant faction, the Know-Nothings, also called the Order of the Star-Spangled Banner, gained prominence. They led a national campaign against immigrant workers and Catholics, who they felt were having an adverse impact on American cultural norms. They advocated extending the length of time it took immigrants to become U.S. citizens in an attempt to discourage non–western Europeans. At one point, the Know-Nothings were able to control state legislatures in several northeastern states. Eventually their cause lost momentum as more pressing national issues, such as the Civil War, took priority.

After the Civil War, the focus on naturalization privileges shifted to centralized control over immigration. The first immigration office in the federal government was created in 1864. The agency was to be formed under the Department of State, led by a commissioner of immigration, who would serve a term of four years. During this period, the agency was responsible for interviewing and denying entrance to individuals convicted of political offenses, lunatics, imbeciles, and persons likely to become public charges. The agency was also authorized to create an immigration fund, based on fees to be collected from each immigrant who entered via maritime ports.

Between 1870 and 1920 approximately 26 million people came to the United States, exceeding the total population of 1850. It is during these fifty years that the romanticized image of the immigrant emerged in the United States. At this time most immigrants, the majority of whom were European, entered the United States at New York Harbor and were processed at Ellis Island. It was not until later in the twentieth century that immigrants would be predominantly from Asia and Latin America, dramatically changing the demographics of immigrant groups and the United States generally.

As the demand for cheap labor grew, so did Chinese immigration. On the West Coast, resentment of Chinese immigrants mounted. In 1881 the California legislature declared a legal holiday to conduct anti-Chinese rallies (Ong Hing 1993). Petitions were sent to Congress to do something about was perceived as the Chinese problem. And in 1882 Congress passed the Chinese Exclusion Act, which put an end to immigration from China and prevented the naturalization of those Chinese immigrants already in the United States. Historians maintain that these efforts to eliminate Chinese nationals were an attempt to ease worker competition between immigrant and American workers.

In 1888 the Ford Commission was established to study the growing immigration problem. This commission found that countries were sending thousands of their paupers and insane persons to America, that immigration through Canada was a problem, that immigration laws were being violated, and that the 1882 Chinese Exclusion Act was simply too difficult to enforce. The commission attributed these problems to the way in which immigration laws were implemented. It recommended strengthening authority over the enforcement of immigrant laws. On March 3, 1891, Congress codified federal control of immigration by establishing the Office of the Superintendent of Immigration. The agency was subsequently moved into the Department of the Treasury.

At the turn of the century, several laws solidified the duties of this newly formed immigration bureau. The Act of 1893, for example, changed the title Superintendent of Immigration to Commissioner-General of Immigration, giving the commissioner more authority. In 1899 new statutes were promulgated that provided for stricter control of immigrants entering the country through maritime ports. In 1900 agency headquarters were set up in Washington, D.C., as were inspection centers at important ports of entry.

In 1903 the agency was moved again, this time into the Department of Labor. In 1906 naturalization duties were assigned to the immigration bureau, making it responsible for both immigration and naturalization. According to INS records, this arrangement continued for seven years before the agency was separated again in 1914. As the agency grew larger and as laws became more complex, it became more difficult for the agency to meet its assigned objectives. Annual reports began to document problems in enforcing immigration policies.

Anti-immigrant sentiment reemerged at the beginning of the twentieth century. During World War I, American resentment of immigrants from southern and eastern Europe grew. The Immigration Act of 1917 hardened preceding restrictions and added new classes of immigrants deemed inadmissible. Among the immigrants denied admission to the United States were illiterates, persons of constitutional inferiority, individuals entering for immoral purposes, chronic alcoholics, stowaways, vagrants, and persons who had suffered attacks of insanity. The act also stipulated that persons coming from designated areas (primarily Asia and the Pacific Islands) would be denied admission into the United States.

By 1918 a labor shortage had developed in the United States. Congress and the immigration agency were encouraged by business interests to secure cheap workers to fill labor needs. This program allowed the agency to directly recruit Mexican workers and place them in jobs in both the agriculture and railroad sectors.

When World War I ended, anti-immigrant sentiment surfaced again. Opinion polls indicated that many Americans felt that a large influx of European immigrants coming from war-destroyed areas would result in a decrease in available jobs. Furthermore, anti-immigrant sentiment toward eastern Europeans once again escalated. Based on both economic and nativistic motives, in 1921 and 1924 Congress enacted the Quota Limit Laws, which marked the beginning of specific restrictions on the entry of certain groups into the United States, among them eastern Europeans, Africans, Australians, and Asians. There were fewer restrictions on immigration from western European countries.

The passage of these laws created another unanticipated objective for the INS. Because sailors had a legal right to go ashore, many European immigrants denied access by the Quota Limit Laws were entering by means of "deserting" from ocean vessels. As the Mexican borders became a point of entry for Europeans who could not otherwise gain admittance because of a lack of proper documentation or because they were illiterate, the smuggling industry grew. In 1922, 309,556 such individuals entered through Mexico, and in 1923, the figure almost doubled to 600,000 (U.S. Congress 1985).

To address the problem of border entries, Congress established the first Border Patrol unit; immigration officers began to patrol the Mexican and Canadian borders on horseback. Interestingly, migration from Mexico was not severely restricted during this period because many Mexican immigrants did not stay in the United States permanently. That is, migration from Mexico was a back-and-forth phenomenon. In 1911, however, the Mexican Revolution led to the first large wave of Mexican migration; records indicate that a quarter of a million legal immigrants eventually entered the country. This wave of migration established the social and community networks of Mexican migration today.

During the Depression, one-third of all Americans were unemployed, causing the emergence of popular and political sentiment against Mexican nationals. President Herbert Hoover insisted that Mexican immigrants took jobs from Americans and were responsible for the depression (Sanchez 1993). The California legislature enacted a law making it illegal to hire undocumented Mexican immigrants. As a result, more than one-third of the members of the Mexican community in the United States were repatriated or deported, either forced or voluntary. It is estimated that five hundred thousand Mexican nationals and Mexican-American citizens were repatriated (Sanchez 1993; Ruiz 1998). This period of mass deportation of Mexican nationals and Mexican Americans would be repeated on a larger scale in the 1950s.

In 1933 the Bureau of Immigration and the Bureau of Naturalization were consolidated, forming what is today known as the Immigration and Naturalization Service. The consolidation of the two agencies was an effort to ensure greater uniformity of immigration procedures. For example, immigration officials had complained that naturalization procedures were not uniform among examiners; some immigrants were denied for petty reasons, while other immigrants of the same status were approved. The newly formed INS began to create a comprehensive set of standardized guidelines for its employees.

During World War II, American resentment of Asian Pacific immigrants escalated. It was felt that Japanese immigrants and Japanese Americans posed a great threat to national security, and the INS was moved to the Department of Justice, where it remains today. Also during this period, Congress passed the Alien Registration Act, requiring that the INS register and fingerprint all immigrants considered "government subversives." As World War II deepened and public sentiment against Japanese immigrants and Japanese Americans grew more severe, the INS became responsible for the apprehension, custody, internment, parole, and deportation of these "subversives."

In response to the labor shortage caused by the war effort, public attitudes toward Mexican and other immigrant workers shifted once again. Records indicate that in 1946 the INS, with the assistance of the Department of Labor, recruited approximately 82,000 laborers through the War Manpower Commission Act to increase agricultural and industrial employment. Under this act, 43,088 Mexicans, 9,589 Jamaicans, 5,052 Bahamians, 2,187 Barbadians, 669 Newfoundlanders, and 160 Hondurans were registered.

Starting in 1942, agricultural employers were able to secure cheap Mexican labor on a seasonal basis. The United States, in conjunction with the Mexican government, began a contracted worker system called the Bracero Program. The program granted temporary worker status to Mexican laborers on a season-by-season basis for agricultural needs. The program has been criticized for its abuses of Mexican workers and has been compared to a slave labor program. Employers had power and discretion over pay, working and sleeping conditions, and food. The program was halted in the early 1960s by both the U.S. and Mexican governments. As a result of the onerous conditions suffered by the braceros, immigrants chose to enter the country illegally to seek employment on their own.

When World War II ended, the role of the INS changed to accommodate the needs of displaced persons. Records indicate that the INS processed 205,000 displaced persons from Europe. The INS had to change its image from that of an enforcement agency, established a few years earlier, to that of an immigrant-friendly agency.

As the Korean War escalated in the early 1950s, labor needs again became an issue for policy makers. Subsequently, Public Law 78, which allowed Mexican nationals to be recruited for employment, was reinstated. The law passed with little opposition, and the INS returned to the practice of recruiting and delivering workers to agricultural employers. By the time this labor system ended in 1964, the INS had supplied approximately three million Mexican workers to growers and ranchers in the Southwest (Calavita 1992).

In 1952 a preference plan for skilled immigrants was developed. Admission into the country was based on employment skills in relation to current labor needs. As a result, the INS became responsible for filing visa applications, allocating visas according to the new system, and using new preference categories for immigrants. The INS was also responsible for creating a central index of the names of all immigrants admitted. In 1955, in another attempt to improve service, the INS was reorganized. Regional offices were established and assigned managerial and supervisory responsibilities over field activities.

In 1954, during a recession, public sentiment once again turned against Mexican immigrants. The INS began removing Mexican nationals through an involuntary departure procedure known as Operation Wetback.[3] Indicative of yet another change in attitude toward the Mexican national, according to the INS, apprehensions and deportations reached 1.3 million in 1954; by 1959 approximately 3.8 million Mexican nationals were deported (Garcia 1980).[4] Operation Wetback is one of the darkest and most dangerous examples of what can occur because of anti-Mexican sentiment. It elicited criticism from both sides of the border, and Congress eventually enacted the Migrant Labor Agreements. Coordinated with Mexico, the objective of the binational agreements was to work together to recruit laborers and to promote more humane treatment of undocumented immigrants.

During the 1950s, INS enforcement and investigation procedures were reorganized to monitor migration to urban areas. Undocumented immigrants fleeing agricultural labor in pursuit of better-paying U.S. jobs, such as those in the manufacturing and industrial sectors, were migrating to cities. District offices were set up in large city centers, and raids and sting operations acquired greater importance in the agency. This created yet another surge in the volume of investigative cases the INS was processing.

In line with other laws passed in the 1960s, such as the Civil Rights Act, the Voting Rights Act, and the Equal Opportunity Act, the 1965 Immigration Act provided opportunities to individuals who were previously denied immigration rights based on ethnicity. The act lifted the ban on certain immigrants previously barred from admission and created a system of family preference that made it easier for immigrants to bring in family members. Simply put, the result of this act was that immigrants who were previously denied admission, especially Asians and Latin Americans, now began entering the United States in significant numbers. Not surprisingly, the Immigration Act resulted in another expansion of INS responsibilities.

Civil and political unrest in Central America and East Asia created new surges in refugee admissions. During the 1960s and early 1970s, a significant number of refugees were admitted under special programs outside standard refugee provisions. INS agents inexperienced in refugee policy were brought from various sectors of the agency to assist with the process.

In the 1970s the commissioner of immigration complained that the agency's record-keeping system, processing of applications, and service to the public needed improvement. This was largely due to the new responsibilities in urban enforcement, refugee processing, and immigrant services. The INS implemented new automation, record-keeping, and processing programs. Criticism of U.S. immigration policy (and subsequently of the role of the INS) grew stronger.

Immigration Policies: The Past Twenty Years

In the 1980s rates of undocumented immigration escalated. The U.S. government responded by reducing the economic lure of jobs. By denying employment, policy makers assumed immigration would diminish drastically. The Select Commission on Immigration and Refugee Policy appointed to assess immigration issues affirmed: "We recommend closing the back door to undocumented/illegal migration [and] opening the front door a little more to accommodate legal migration in the interests of this country" (Muñoz 1990: 1).

In 1986 the Immigration Reform and Control Act was enacted. The overall objective of irca was to decrease the number of undocumented immigrants in the United States by implementing two provisions: employer sanctions and legalization. The employer sanctions provision was intended to end the economic lure for immigrants who come to the United States seeking employment. The legalization provision legalized undocumented immigrants already in the United States, thereby reducing the total number of undocumented individuals. Overall, the policy resulted in the processing of more than 3 million immigrants seeking legalized status. In addition, the ins took responsibility for informing over 7 million employers of the provisions and penalties of the new law.

In 1990 immigration policy was once again overhauled, to address legal. and undocumented immigration. Under the Immigration Act of 1990, the number of immigrants under the "flexible cap" was increased to 675,000, and funding was increased to hire an additional one thousand Border Patrol officers. Agency guidelines on the exclusion, naturalization, and deportation of undocumented immigrants were rewritten.

Almost ten years after passage of IRCA, undocumented immigration again became the target of popular reform initiatives, particularly in California, Texas, Arizona, and Florida, where immigrant communities flourish. In 1994 California passed perhaps the most controversial ballot measure, Proposition 187, also known as the "Save Our State Initiative," to address the cost of illegal immigration.

Although Proposition 187 was eventually found unconstitutional, it set the stage for welfare reform as a means to decrease illegal and legal immigration. In 1996 the Personal Responsibility Act was passed. This act restricted legal immigrants from receiving social services and barred legal immigrants from receiving food stamps and Social Security. It also broadened restrictions on federal, state, and local benefits for undocumented immigrants, who were already barred from most forms of welfare. Also in 1996, Congress increased criminal penalties for immigration-related offenses. The INS was allocated funds to hire more enforcement personnel and to enhance enforcement authority over street-level immigration operations.

Most recently, critics of the agency contend that service activities, such as the processing of immigrants, are incompatible with the INS's expanded enforcement activities. As a result, a plan is under way to restructure the INS. This plan will separate the INS into the Bureau of Immigration Services and the Bureau of Immigration Enforcement. Furthermore, another bracero, or temporary worker, program is being considered. President George W. Bush and President Vicente Fox are considering the merits of this program, which has the support of several governors of southwestern states.

BELOW IS A TIME LINE of the major immigration policies carried out by the INS during the past eighty years that have had a significant effect on Mexican immigrants. These policies were motivated by the economic and popular whims of the time, with little consideration of the agency's capacity to implement them or of how they would change lives.

1920s The Quota Limit Laws—Ethnic quotas were placed on the admissions of immigrants entering the United States.

1930s The Great Repatriations—More than 500,000 Mexicans were repatriated to Mexico.

1940s Bracero Program—The recruitment of millions of Mexicans to fill labor needs.

1950s Operation Wetback—The deportation of 3 million Mexicans.

1960s 1965 Immigration Act—The liberalization of immigration policy to accommodate more immigration. Lifted ethnic quotas placed on previously barred immigrants from Latin America and Asia.

1980s Immigration Reform and Control Act—The most comprehensive policy created to control undocumented immigration, including punishing employers who knowingly hired illegal immigrants and changing the status of immigrants who were illegal to legal.

1996 1996 Immigration Act—Policies created to end social services afforded to immigrants, both legal and illegal, as well stricter penalties for smuggling activities. Also increased manpower and resources at border areas.

2000s? New Bracero Program—Policies are being considered to reintroduce a program to recruit Mexican laborers.

Summary

The immigration policy process has had profound implications for the size and scope of the INS. In an attempt to improve agency performance, the INS has been moved from the Department of the Treasury to the Department of Labor to the Department of Justice. The immigration and naturalization bureaus were also consolidated to improve standardization. However, consolidating these agencies did not improve uniformity.

In fact, the agency today continues to be criticized for lack of standardization and discretionary decisions made by INS bureaucrats. Ironically, in another attempt to improve agency effectiveness, the agency is currently being separated.

Popular sentiment has also resulted in the agency having to change its organizational mission. At certain points in history, the INS was mainly a service agency, such as when it processed immigrants displaced after World War II, or an enforcement agency, such as when it kept immigrants out of the country under the provisions of the Quota Limit Laws. The agency has also been an employment agency, facilitating the agricultural needs of employers in the Bracero Program.

Today, studies indicate that many of the enforcement policies, such as increasing border patrol, have had no overall effect on the rate of undocumented immigration into the United States. For instance, immigrants can circumvent the enhanced Border Patrol presence in Texas and California by entering through less patrolled areas, such as the Arizona desert. It is also clear that restrictive laws created to deter undocumented immigration were halted as the need for cheap labor increased.

Another theme throughout this chapter is that immigration policies are hastily created and not well formulated. They are and continue to be dictated by popular and political sentiment. Since immigration policies change quickly and considerably, the policy actors in the INS are left uncertain as to their goals and mandates. Doris Meissner, commissioner of the INS, maintains that public attitudes have shaped the overall size and duties of the agency throughout history. She maintains citizens need to *believe* that the INS can control immigration:

> Public attitudes demand that someone pay attention to immigration laws. I believe immigration laws survive only if people believe in rules that can be properly enforced. Ironically, immigration laws and their enforcement are what allow us to remain open to immigration as a country. Americans want a sense of confidence and [want to know] that the process is not chaotic. (Pers. com. October 1998)

Meissner further states that immigration reforms are unclear and that few policy makers agree on what should be done. Given this ambivalence, it is difficult to run the agency.

Chapter Three

"We Aren't Sexy Enough"

WORKING CONDITIONS AT THE INS

WORKING CONDITIONS AT THE INS influence how the public perceives the agency, how programs are developed and funded by Congress, and how the INS carries out policies despite what appear to be illogical mandates. Overall, the INS maintains that it has two organizational missions, enforcement and service. Because these missions are intertwined, it is difficult to separate them.

This chapter is divided into two sections. The first provides descriptive data: funding, demographics, and occupational structure. The second section, based on interviews with INS representatives as well as newspaper articles and studies of the agency, describes some of the constraints and obstacles INS representatives confront when carrying out immigration policies.

Agency Description

Organizationally, those engaged in the service function of the INS deal directly with immigrants who wish to come to the United States either temporarily or permanently or who want to become legal residents or American citizens. Those engaged in enforcement prevent undocumented immigrants from entering the country illegally and find and remove undocumented immigrants who are living or working in the United States.

Responsibilities under the service category include naturalization, training, and legal proceedings. "Naturalization" is defined as the conferring of citizenship status on legal immigrants. Training includes keeping representatives up-to-date on the ever-changing status of immigration laws. Legal proceedings involve the processing of immigrants who may challenge previous immigration decisions.

Responsibilities defined as enforcement are investigations, antismuggling activities, detention and deportation, inspections, and patrolling the border. The investigations unit monitors and inspects places of employment for unauthorized workers in the interior region of the country. Anti-smuggling detects and prosecutes alien smuggling operations. Detention and deportation takes criminals and undocumented immigrants into custody pending proceedings to determine their status, such as removal from the United States. Inspections screens all travelers arriving in the United States by air, land, or sea, monitoring approximately two hundred fifty ports of entry. Border Patrol agents monitor the border region for illegal entries.

Housed under the Department of Justice, the INS is headed by a federal commissioner. There are thirty-three districts and twenty-one Border Patrol sectors throughout the United States, in addition to offices outside of the country. Nine detention facilities known as Service Processing Centers (SPCs) are in operation, in addition to state and local jails used by the agency.

The commissioner oversees the general counsel and congressional relations. Four associate commissioners oversee programs: field operations, policy planning, and management. In terms of area operations, the country is divided into three regions: west, east, and central.

Recently, proposals to restructure the agency have been drafted. The general intent of these proposals is to separate the two functions of the agency, service and enforcement, while keeping them under the direction of one commissioner. The enforcement and service functions will each have their own director. Ideally, enforcement will still be responsible for illegal immigration activities at the border, ports of entry, and the interior United States. Immigration services will continue to process benefits, such as employment authorization, green card renewals or replacement, and petitions for family- and employment-based immigration. On November 14, 2001, the INS released its reorganization plan, stipulating that "the separation of these functions, while retaining a single agency head to ensure appropriate coordination, balance and policy leadership, will help improve the efficiency and effectiveness of the agency and, in turn, the nation's immigration system" (U.S. Department of Justice 2001). However, during interviews, respondents overwhelmingly opposed it.

FISCAL GROWTH

Moneys recently have been allocated to improve the INS. According to the INS executive budget summary, the current budget allocates moneys to expedite the time required to process immigrants or grant citizenship. It also makes provisions for upgrading pay; $10.1 million has been allocated to

Table 5. *FY2000 INS total obligations (including carryovers) by program within "Enforcement" and "Benefits"*

Program	Obligations	% Enforcement	% Overall
"ENFORCEMENT"			
Inspections	$479,893,300.00	16.99%	10.90%
Border Patrol	$1,076,645,082.00	38.11%	24.45%
Investigations	$340,961,228.00	12.07%	7.74%
Detention & Deportation	$913,704,265.00	32.34%	20.75%
Intelligence	$4,023,680.00	0.50%	0.32%
Total "Enforcement"	$2,825,227,555.00	100.00%	64.17%
"BENEFITS"		% BENEFIT	
Adjudications & Naturalization	$486,474,506.00	30.84%	11.05%
International Affairs	$100,828,072.00	6.39%	2.29%
Training	$22,997,763.00	1.46%	0.52%
Data & Communications	$396,703,627.00	25.15%	9.01%
Information & Records	$197,298,723.00	12.51%	4.48%
Construction & Engineering	$117,909,629.00	7.47%	2.68%
Legal Proceedings	$84,810,875.00	5.38%	1.93%
Management & Administration	$170,479,425.00	10.81%	3.87%
Total "Benefits"	$1,577,502,620.00	100.00%	35.83%
Total INS	$4,402,730,175.00		100.00%

Note: the separation of program obligations into "Enforcement" and "Benefits" is based solely on Congress's segregation of appropriated funds into "Enforcement and Border Affairs" and "Citizenship & Benefits, Support and Program Direction." It must be recognized that the "split" was not definitive, in that some of the expenses under "Benefits" are for shared services that support both enforcement and benefits activities (e.g. personnel staffing, financial accounting, legal support, etc.). In addition, Management & Administration includes District Directors and staffs that support both enforcement and benefits activities. There is NO financial accounting that provides a perfect distinction between enforcement, benefits, and shared services at this time. Prepared by Budget Reports and Analysis Branch
Source: INS Financial Accounting and Control System (FACS) sent April 2000.

ensure greater professionalism in the workforce. The agency was also funded to upgrade its technological efforts, such as adding more computers and remote video surveillance systems along the borders.

Table 5 and Figures 2 and 3 provide actual budget numbers for FY2000 and the allocation for activities and programs. Clearly, immigration re-

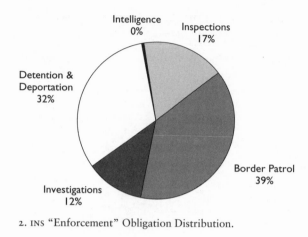

2. INS "Enforcement" Obligation Distribution.

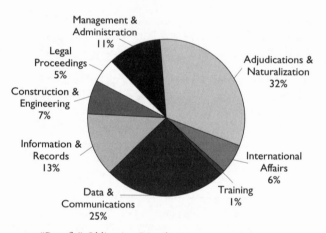

3. INS "Benefit" Obligation Distribution.

form was an important issue during the past decade. Since 1993 there has been a 219 percent increase in the overall budget. On the whole, enforcement policies have taken greater priority than have service policies. For instance, since 1993 there has been a 175 percent increase in Border Patrol personnel alone. Not surprisingly, popular sentiment demanded an emphasis on enforcement activities over service activities; 64 percent of the budget is allocated to enforcement policies, with the remaining 36 percent to service or benefits. Service functions are funded in part by user fees paid by immigrants.

DEMOGRAPHICS

As of November 2000 there were approximately 30,500 INS employees, of whom 70 percent are male. Salaries vary depending on length of employment and position. In general, the majority of INS employees are in the professional, administrative, and "other" categories. The INS places the Border Patrol under the category "other."

The demographic breakdown of the INS may shed light on perceptions by the public, particularly the Latino public. More than half of all employees are Anglo. More than one-fourth of the INS workforce define themselves as Hispanic. This demographic characteristic is important for several reasons. First, this makes the INS one of the largest, if not the largest, federal employer of Hispanics. Second, it appears that the agency hires more Hispanic employees because of the large number of Mexican immigrants with whom it deals. Hispanic INS employees, however, are found primarily in the Border Patrol. This suggests that Mexican immigrants are more likely to deal with Hispanic INS representatives when they are enforcing immigration law than when they are providing services to immigrants.[1]

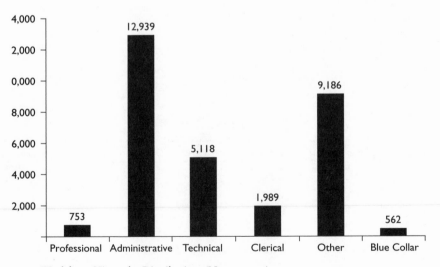

4. INS Workforce Hierarchy Distribution. (N = 30,500)

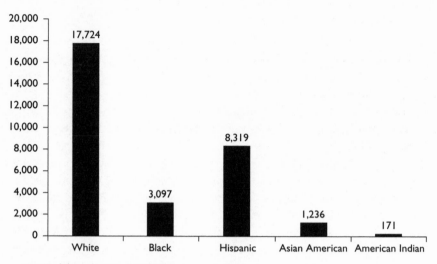

5. INS Workforce by Ethnicity. (N = 30,500)

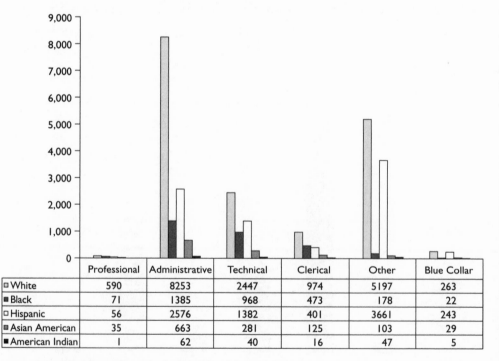

	Professional	Administrative	Technical	Clerical	Other	Blue Collar
☐ White	590	8253	2447	974	5197	263
▪ Black	71	1385	968	473	178	22
☐ Hispanic	56	2576	1382	401	3661	243
▪ Asian American	35	663	281	125	103	29
▪ American Indian	1	62	40	16	47	5

6. INS Workforce Hierarchy by Ethnicity. (N = 30,500)

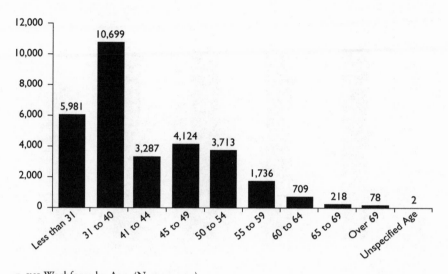

7. INS Workforce by Age. (N = 30,500)

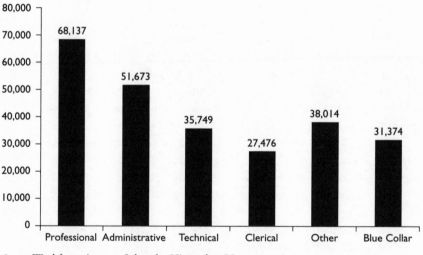

8. INS Workforce Average Salary by Hierarchy. (N = 30,500)

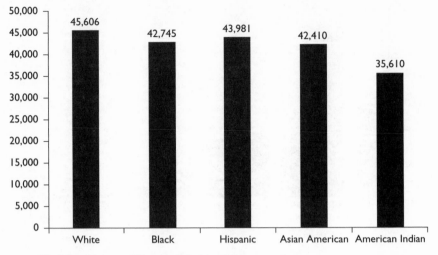

9. INS Workforce Average Salary by Ethnicity. (N = 30,500)

Constraints and Obstacles

PUBLIC PERCEPTION

According to interviews conducted with INS representatives, the agency's working conditions greatly influence the way in which it carries out its mandates. Although, as stated earlier, the interview responses do not represent the views of all INS employees, they provide insight into the frustrations and constraints experienced by our respondents.

The respondents maintained that the general public does not understand what the INS does. One upper-level INS representative stated, "People want to control immigration when it is faceless, but when someone has a friend who needs immigration help, people have no problem calling us for assistance or asking us to make exceptions." Contrary perceptions of what the INS can and cannot do result in criticism of the agency, which in turn influences employees' morale.

Respondents feel that because the public does not understand the agency's duties, the organization is held accountable for unrelated directives. For instance, undocumented immigration to the United States is the result of geopolitical and international forces outside the agency's control. Yet the INS is responsible for decreasing the level of "undocumented" immigration. In short, the agency representatives work in an environment clouded by ambiguity and the need to deal with impossible and conflicting mandates. For instance, they explained that if programs are not well understood by the public the agency may need to use precious resources and time clarifying them. Conversely, if the agency's objectives are clearly perceived or programs have been relatively consistent, the agency can rely on its reputation and provide more efficient assistance.

Public understanding of what an agency does is crucial to its success. In an effort to cultivate a positive image, the INS holds classes that are open to the public to explain its activities. On March 21, 1999, the *Los Angeles Times* published the following story:

> In two-hour sessions over seven weeks, Diaz and about 20 other people—college students, teachers, retirees—are introduced to topics ranging from anti-smuggling intelligence gathering to the use of deadly force in making arrests. . . . Besides the obvious public relations value, the classes offer residents a chance to peer more closely into the workings of an agency that is a prominent, often controversial, fixture of daily life along the U.S.-Mexico border.

Respondents overwhelmingly stated that the press selectively magnifies negative events, which makes the agency look insensitive. One respondent said, "Only the bad things get printed; the good stuff never does, but what sells papers?" Recent attention to immigration issues in the press may fuel the public's perception that the agency is ineffective. Respondents maintain that a more careful examination would reveal that the INS is a government agency that works hard to enforce immigration laws while also paying close attention to civil and social rights. One INS respondent maintained that the Border Patrol generates the most attention and is perhaps considered the "sexiest" of all INS activities.

Respondents also believe that politicians portray the INS as incapable of fulfilling its assigned duties in order to avoid criticism by the public. The high rate of undocumented immigration and the long time it takes to process immigrants are used as examples of the agency's ineffectiveness. Governmental officials continue to express such sentiments in the media, fueling this perception in the minds of the public.

THE DUAL MISSION

INS representatives maintain that they must work to overcome their conflicting missions. For example, representatives on the service side must make immigrants feel that the INS is a safe place to seek assistance, whereas representatives on the enforcement side must perpetuate its image as tough on undocumented immigration.

It is difficult to assess just how the agency's dual mission affects potential immigrants across the United States. In 1990, for example, the Tomás Rivera Center (TRC), a national Latino policy research institute, surveyed approximately five hundred Latinos in Los Angeles. In one section, pollsters wanted to know why persons eligible to change from illegal to legal status were not applying. The data showed that among eligible Latinos not applying for legal status, a full 53 percent were afraid of the INS (Solis 1990). Another study conducted by the National Association for Latino Elected Officials (NALEO) confirmed that the INS's enforcement image has a deterrent effect on immigrants asking for immigration assistance (NALEO 1989). These studies indicate that immigrants are not likely to go to an agency for assistance if they have been taught to avoid it.

According to respondents, their dual mission influences greatly their ability to carry out policies, particularly when servicing immigrants. A July 31, 1993, article in the *Los Angeles Times* illustrates the dilemma immigrants, and therefore the INS, confront:

> Antonio Martinez read the letter from the Immigration and Naturalization Service several times, and got an uneasy feeling each time. After two years of battling the INS to legalize his status so he could remain here with his American wife and daughter, the offer seemed too good to be true. Come to the Federal Building, bring some identification and we'll give you a work permit good for a year, the letter said. How can the letter not be authentic, asked Martinez's wife, Ariel, a Chula Vista native. It was written on INS stationery and said Martinez qualified under the "*Immigration and Nationality Act of 1993.*"
>
> At the end, Ariel's optimism and belief in the INS' credibility won out. On July 20, Martinez, his wife and the couple's 18-month old daughter drove to the INS office downtown to pick up his permit. But instead of being welcomed by their adopted country, Martinez and dozens of others were promptly arrested and deported.

These types of operations perpetuate the idea that the agency cannot be trusted. This is ironic, since Latino immigrants are supposed to migrate the "right way," yet activities such as the one described above only serve to discourage trust in the agency.

It also appears that the agency's dual mission, enforcement and service, may not be dual at all. Rather, according to respondents, the enforcement

mission dictates other agency activities and takes priority over other duties. When respondents were asked how they saw the agency—as more of
an enforcement or more of a service agency—*most* commented that service had a lower priority. One person remarked, "I think that the agency
is schizophrenic between whether it is supposed to keep people out or facilitate the process of coming into the United States. Enforcement seems
to be the priority and service a later agenda." It will be interesting to see
if separating the agency will in fact eradicate many of the dual mission
problems or if it is simply another recommendation with which INS bureaucrats will have to contend.

INTERNAL CONSTRAINTS

Respondents stated that poor communication styles characterize the
agency's working conditions. It is particularly important for upper management in the INS to remain in touch with events in the field. The INS's
communication style is described as highly bureaucratic, and respondents
maintain that it affects their ability to carry out policies. When respondents were asked to describe the communication process from upper management down to the street level, the process was typically described as
"out of touch."

Researchers from the GAO (1990) found that the communication process in the INS is heavily bureaucratic, with a heavy reliance on interoffice
memorandums. A survey of INS managers revealed that the policy information they eventually received was outdated and poorly disseminated
and that instructions for policy implementation were unclear and incom-
plete for managers (GAO 1991). One respondent contended, "If there is a
problem, we cannot act on it until [we] get back a memo." She went on
to say that the link between passage of a new policy and educating those
responsible for its implementation is sorely lacking. INS respondents also
commented on the highly bureaucratic environment of the agency and the
difficulty they have encountered in getting assistance or clarification on
immigration policy.

INS respondents also voiced concern that the agency lacks stature at the
federal level. In fact, one former INS federal commissioner referred to his
agency as the "ugly stepchild of the Justice Department." A 1991 study
criticized the INS's overall leadership skills, recommending stronger leadership to balance the demanding roles of enforcement and service and
finding that weak management systems and inconsistent leadership styles
have allowed serious problems in the INS to go unresolved (GAO 1991).

Respondents also criticized the ever-changing organizational directives of newly appointed administrators and leaders of the agency. They maintained that as new elected officials come into office, so do new ideas for the agency. Respondents, particularly those at the federal level, maintain that it is difficult to develop administrative procedures when implementing poorly designed policies. Poor leadership does not cause administrative inadequacies, yet politicians are quick to blame the INS leadership. In a recent article on the leadership of the INS, Doris Miessner, its federal commissioner, was described as follows:

> Outside observers of the INS portray Meissner as a decent and committed woman trapped in an impossible system. Even after nearly five years on the job, Meissner is still confronted with autonomous fiefdoms in the INS regional offices that operate on the principle that commissioners come and go but the bureaucracy is forever. (*USA Today*, April 8, 1998)

ABUSE OF DISCRETION AND MISCONDUCT

INS representatives stated that they are criticized by the public, particularly Latino interest groups, for exercising too much discretion in enforcement decisions and not enough discretion in service decisions. For instance, there are a multitude of stories describing INS enforcement agents as overzealous when dealing with undocumented immigrants. Newspapers frequently report instances in which the INS has raided points of employment without proper authorization and harassed Mexican Americans based on their appearance. The *Los Angeles Times* ran the following article on August 14, 1992:

> Temecula—The city previously filed—and lost—a lawsuit against the U.S. Immigration and Naturalization Service, which oversees the Border Patrol, claiming its policy for high-speed chases was ambiguous and left too many life-and-death decisions to the discretion of the pursuing officers. The suit was prompted by the deaths of six people in June.

Meissner reported in an interview that she knew there were abuses of discretion and misconduct in the agency. However, proving and punishing these cases is difficult. Further, because fellow INS employees may not feel comfortable exposing their coworkers or because victims of such abuses are not likely to report them given their illegal status, many cases of abuse go unreported.

During October 1999, a group of community leaders and I met with Meissner regarding the treatment of Mexicans and Mexican Americans by the INS in southern Arizona. Activists described an INS that continually abused and insulted individuals and instilled fear in the community. One leader described INS agents entering restaurants and harassing families. Another described being harassed while waiting for a family member at a train station. Meissner maintained that these activities are strongly discouraged and that they interfere with the agency's attempt to develop a positive image.

On the enforcement side, respondents expressed frustration. INS agents contend that not all immigrants are fearful of the agency. One agent noted, "Immigrants are circumventing the system; some may be fearful. However, they get coping skills to avoid the agency; they do not have to change their lives." Although enforcement is continually characterized as an ineffective and inefficient approach to curbing undocumented immigration, the INS continues to fund enforcement disproportionately, relative to the service side. When it comes to enforcing immigration laws, both sides have valid observations. There are immigrants who fear the agency, and there are immigrants who have learned to avoid contact with the agency.

Respondents maintained that inexperienced INS agents display much lower levels of discretion than more experienced agents. That is, rookie agents feel that they constantly have to look to their supervisors for input before implementing policies. As agents become more experienced, the level of discretion drastically increases. Discretion is an indication of an experienced agent.

Conversely, service representatives stated that they are not afforded enough discretion in decision making and that it is not realistic to work in an environment where such rigidity exits. A *Denver Post* article of November 13, 1998, exemplifies the rigidity associated with the INS in service decisions:

> The Immigration and Naturalization Service held her [an immigrant] in the New Orleans Parish Prison for a week and then put her on a plane back to Germany. She was treated like a criminal because she had made a mistake in her immigration process. While awaiting adjustment of her status to permanent resident, she . . . had gone to Germany to visit her parents—which no one had told [her] was against the rules.

Because immigrants come from diverse backgrounds and circumstances, it is difficult to have standardized procedures for processing them. INS respondents on the service side expressed frustration that they are not allowed to make decisions based on an immigrant's unique circumstances. For instance, recent laws make any legal immigrant with a felony ineligible for citizenship, even if that felony was a youthful indiscretion for which the individual had already completed his or her punishment. Respondents felt this was unfair and that they should be given more discretion. They also maintained that such a rule was an example of Congress's attempt to appease constituents without fully understanding INS operations.

Summary

It is clear from the interviewees' responses that the agency's working conditions affect the overall immigration policy process. For instance, activities on the enforcement side undermine efforts on the service side. Furthermore, because the agency is responsible for directives that are misunderstood by outsiders, it is susceptible to criticism. Respondents believe, for example, that the public as well as politicians use the agency as a scapegoat for the large numbers of undocumented immigrants.

Respondents are aware that there are problems in the agency. Abuses by unscrupulous agents can go unreported while service representatives are constrained from making decisions based on their own expertise. Finally, improving the agency requires significant resources and personpower. For instance, it would take an extraordinary number of INS representatives to streamline the processing of immigrants. The task of changing working conditions at the INS is challenging. I turn now to how these working conditions influence policy implementation.

Chapter Four

The Immigration Reform and Control Act

A CASE STUDY

IRCA IS THE MOST COMPREHENSIVE policy ever developed to decrease undocumented immigration. I concentrate here on the implementation of IRCA by the INS in Los Angeles, which processed the largest number of IRCA immigrants in the United States. Of the 3.1 million immigrants in the United States who applied for amnesty, 1.1 million resided in Los Angeles. The findings of this case study demonstrate that despite the agency's overwhelming emphasis on enforcement, it was more successful in carrying out its service mission. These findings are especially important given the current debate in Congress over whether to initiate a legalization policy similar to IRCA and given the current emphasis on policing rather than assistance.

Background

During the the 1970s, the number of deportable aliens apprehended by the INS was steadily growing. At the same time, the number of immigrants being admitted into the United States legally was also increasing, with the result that the INS was not able to handle the volume of work. Criticism from both the public and the Congress ensued.

Legislators hypothesized that one way to reduce the number of undocumented immigrants flowing into the United States, especially into cities, was to eliminate one of the "pull" factors, job opportunities. When newly arrived undocumented immigrants learned that they were not able to find employment, it was proposed, they would inform people in their country of origin, and undocumented immigration would decline (Rolph 1990).

A bill sponsored during the Carter administration called for punishing employers who knowingly hired undocumented workers. The proposal failed because critics of immigration legislation claimed that it was not supported by factual analysis and that other alternatives to curb illegal immigration had not been adequately examined (Montwieler 1986).

In 1978 the Select Commission on Immigration and Refugee Policy was formed to study immigration and refugee laws. After several years, the commission recommended legislation that penalized employers for hiring undocumented immigrants, as well as legalization or amnesty for certain immigrants who were already in the country illegally. The commission also suggested tougher Border Patrol measures and a program that would recruit temporary seasonal agricultural workers to fill labor needs.

Within a year of the commission's findings, Sen. Alan Simpson (R-Wyo.) and Rep. Romano Mazzoli (D-Ky.) introduced legislation calling for employer sanctions, permanent residence for some immigrants, and a special program for agricultural workers. Criticisms of the legislation surfaced immediately, because it was not supported by factual evidence; the bill was defeated.

In 1985 Simpson and Mazzoli introduced what was to be their final piece of legislation. This legislation passed because it had a triggered legislation program, a provision that would delay legalization until an appointed commission could determine if employer sanctions were acceptable and actually reduced the number of undocumented immigrants (Montwieler 1986). The legislation also stipulated that the GAO should determine if employer sanctions were discriminatory in practice. If they were found to be discriminatory, Congress would halt the practice.

In 1986 the Immigration Reform and Control Act was enacted. My respondents maintained that the real objectives of IRCA were not to encourage legalization for undocumented immigrants living in this country, or individuals living in the "shadow society," but rather border control. Elizabeth Rolph, a researcher, elaborates:

> Although IRCA paved the way for a large number of undocu-
> mented residents to achieve legal status, its primary mission was
> border control. . . . After almost a decade of debate, they turned to
> the traditional strategy—a strategy intended to reduce the eco-
> nomic lure of illegal immigration. IRCA was to substantially reduce
> illegal immigration by denying jobs to illegal immigrants. Without
> access to employment, those in the United States illegally would be
> forced to return home. (Rolph 1990: 19)

IRCA is perhaps the best contemporary example of a policy distinguished by contradictory objectives. That is, it made the INS responsible for carrying out a policy that assisted undocumented immigrants to attain legal status while at the same time deterring undocumented immigration. INS representatives encouraged undocumented immigrants to enter INS offices and confess to their undocumented status without fear of punishment. Indicative of this dual and contradictory mission, undocumented immigrants were encouraged to seek assistance from the same agency previously responsible for their apprehension, detention, and deportation. The INS had to change its image so that immigrants would feel assured that district offices were safe places. The INS had to transform itself from "La Migra" to "El Amigo."

To implement employer sanctions, the INS first had to inform employers that it was illegal to hire undocumented immigrants. Employers would be penalized for not examining specified documentation, such as birth certificates, Social Security cards, and passports. The challenge for the INS was to become a regulatory agency, an agency that enforces employment law. The agency received a substantial increase in funding to carry out this mission. Legalization, conversely, allowed undocumented immigrants to change their status from illegal to legal, if they could provide proof that they had lived continuously in the United States since 1982. (See Appendix 1 for the provisions of the IRCA.)

Los Angeles

Before the 1950s Mexican undocumented immigrants were found in rural rather than urban areas. Thereafter, this migration pattern changed dramatically. As jobs became more available in cities, cities drew larger numbers of undocumented immigrants.

Los Angeles is located approximately one hundred miles north of the Mexican border, making it by far the most accessible urban area in the United States able to absorb large infusions of unskilled labor (Rolph 1990). A number of factors influence immigration from Mexico to Los Angeles: (1) an evolving social network; (2) a dramatic population explosion in Latin America; (3) a consistent demand for cheap labor; (4) the weak economies of sending countries; and (5) political unrest throughout Latin America (Pearlstone 1989; Rolph 1990).

The Los Angeles INS district is by far the largest of its kind, consisting of more than two thousand employees, while the national average by district is five hundred employees or fewer. The size of the Los Angeles INS is understandable in light of estimates that the city has the largest undocumented population in the United States. The city relies heavily on undocumented immigrant labor (Morales and Bonilla 1993). For instance, in the 1980s, 15 percent of all manufacturing jobs in Los Angeles were in the apparel industry, with as many as 80 percent of these workers undocumented.

Setting Up Employer Sanctions

After the INS was charged with the implementation of IRCA, it developed several new guidelines and objectives. Between December 1986 and May 1987 the INS targeted employers to educate them regarding the new sanctions. Employers, after being warned by the INS, were to be fined if they continued to hire undocumented workers. With the assistance of the Department of Labor and the Internal Revenue Service, the INS mailed employers a handbook describing the sanctions provisions. The INS was also responsible for the dissemination of information through lectures, job-site visits, and telephone inquiries. After an initial period of eighteen months (ending in June 1988), employers were responsible for enforcing the sanctions provisions, including examining employees' documentation and filling out the required authorization forms. Businesses that traditionally relied on undocumented workers were then targeted for on-site inspections to assess compliance.

Following the implementation of education and outreach, the INS focused on enforcing the law. This was a new practice for the INS enforcement unit. Implementing sanctions meant that the agency assumed more regulatory responsibility in its basic mission. Enforcing the law against businesses proved more difficult than enforcing the law against undocumented immigrants.

One of the most important objectives for the INS in implementing sanctions was maintaining and ensuring rapport with the business community. For example, the INS established what it called "a priority management system." That is, the INS penalized employers only after sending a series of warnings. First- and second-time violators received only moderate penalties, such as letters of warning called notices to fine. According to the respondents, only after the third violation were employers sanctioned as stipulated by IRCA.

The Los Angeles district office used the following strategies to implement sanctions: 60 percent of their investigations resulted from leads, 20 percent from random selection, and 20 percent from targeted industries (Juffras 1991). Furthermore, by law the INS provided businesses with three days' advance warning of worksite and documentation inspections.

The federal commissioner's goal for sanctions was to contact 7 million employers by June 30, 1988.

Nationally, the INS expanded its investigations staff from 875 agents to 1,600 for sanctions-related activities, recruiting heavily from outside the agency. This was an innovative practice. INS investigative staff are usually recruited from the Border Patrol for transfer into the Investigations section. The INS sought to enlist individuals who could perform regulatory roles rather than the traditional roles of investigation and deportation. The INS also transferred staff from other units, such as detention, anti-smuggling, and the Border Patrol (Juffras 1991).

Nationally, the INS required that between July 1987 and June 1988 district offices devote 50 percent of their investigative time to employer education. In Los Angeles, enforcement activities consisted of the following budget allocations: 45 percent of enforcement activities were spent on sanctions, including employer education; 22 percent of the remaining enforcement activities focused on fraud; and 33 percent focused on criminal aliens (Juffras 1991).

Setting Up Legalization or "Amnesty"

IRCA mandated that the legalization process must start on May 5, 1987, or one hundred eighty days after enactment of the law. During these six months, the INS opened legalization offices, hired new employees, and recruited additional staff internally. Some objectives were left up to each INS district to define, such as fees, application and documentation requirements, duration of permissible absence from the country, additional public assistance from which applicants would be barred for five years, and educational requirements. Applicants were granted temporary residence alien (TRA) status; after eighteen months their status was adjusted to that of permanent resident alien (PRA).

Unlike the sanctions provision, legalization was primarily self-funded. The INS charged up to $185 per immigrant processed. These fees were then applied to legalization staff salaries and related costs. In the Los Angeles district, 463 positions handled the estimated 1.2 million applicants expected to apply for legalization; sixteen offices opened in the Los Angeles district (Rolph 1990: 68). Legalization began six months after passage of IRCA.

The hiring of new staff was largely an ad hoc process. The INS drew new personnel from three sources. IRCA allowed up to three hundred retired INS officials to take legalization jobs, typically supervisory positions, for

up to eighteen months. The next group was recruited from INS investigative units, such as examinations, inspections, and deportations. Finally,
two thousand individuals were recruited from outside the agency.

The INS did not make the same investment in staffing for legalization
as it did for sanctions. Legalization assistants and adjudicators, responsible for most of the processing, typically occupied relatively low positions
on the federal pay scale, which reflected lower levels of education and experience. By contrast, new special agents recruited for sanctions work
were typically paid more (Juffras 1991: 34). Between 1986 and 1990 the
INS's total service budget rose from $50 million to $133 million, a 166
percent increase. However, this represented only 12 percent of the total
INS budget. By 1990 the INS budget had grown to more than $1.1 billion,
from $574 million in 1986.

Immigrant advocates maintained that amnesty was not created solely
to provide benefits to undocumented immigrants. Rather, legalizing undocumented immigrants, in many ways, was just another enforcement
policy. For instance, one respondent from the Mexican American Legal
Defense and Education Fund (MALDEF) maintained that "legalization"
was yet another enforcement policy in that "it was a way of getting a large
group of immigrants under legalized, policing scrutiny." In the long run
the sanctions program would be an expensive policy to implement because it was ongoing, whereas legalization was a "one-shot-only chance."
Legalizing large numbers of immigrants was a good way to reduce the
costs of enforcing sanctions over the long term. Because of the enforcement benefits of legalization, the respondent explained, immigrant advocacy groups such as MALDEF had considerable lobbying influence during the planning process. For instance, MALDEF had substantial power to
push for more generous acceptance requirements.

Implementing Legalization

All INS respondents felt that legalization rather than sanctions was given
first priority. Respondents repeatedly stated that INS employees' morale
was extremely high during the implementation of legalization. INS representatives felt that overall legalization was an opportunity to provide
benefits to the immigrant community. For example, the head legalization
officer in Los Angeles told me, "The aliens could really benefit from this
program, and it was a chance to change the image of the agency." Respondents contend that there was no such enthusiasm in promoting employer sanctions, and as a result the implementation and success of sanc-

tions suffered. Furthermore, respondents maintained that they were told to be extremely cautious in implementing sanctions. Americans did not want to see employers unduly punished for immigrant problems.

As noted previously, the perception of the INS on the part of the undocumented is not favorable. Why would immigrants go to an agency for assistance that they have historically avoided? The INS hypothesized that there should be places immigrants could visit other than the INS to get processed for legalization. Therefore, groups outside the INS, Qualified Designated Entities (QDEs), would be able to assist immigrants with their needs. These QDEs consisted of churches, unions, and other immigrant advocacy groups. There were approximately eighty QDEs in Los Angeles. They could charge up to $185 per immigrant for their assistance; they were also reimbursed an extra $15 by the INS for each person they assisted (Rolph 1990).

The Catholic Church has historically supported immigrant rights in Los Angeles. Not surprisingly, the QDE used most extensively by immigrants in Los Angeles was the one supported by the church. Respondents recall a significant boost in legalization applications after Los Angeles Cardinal Roger Mahony's public support of legalization. Respondents maintained that Catholic masses became a place for disseminating information about legalization as well the need to apply.

However, a safe place to get one's papers processed did not always coincide with the most efficient place. One respondent from Catholic Charities recalled that during legalization the agency was overwhelmed. He maintained that Catholic Charities did not anticipate the volume of documentation that needed to be processed, filed, and eventually mailed to the INS. He felt that Catholic Charities should have been better prepared for immigrants and their needs. However, he was not sure how small private agencies such as QDEs could prepare sufficiently. Although QDE staff members were immigrant advocates, they were not knowledgeable about immigrant and refugee policies. They were bogged down with time-consuming work, for example, arranging for fingerprinting and photographs, copying documents, helping immigrants to obtain adequate documentation, and tracking the progress of applications at the INS. As it turned out, the INS's legalization sites were better able to deal with immigrant services. All the respondents said they did not anticipate that immigrants would use the INS more than the QDEs. According to INS respondents, the INS processed 86 percent of all legalization applications. One INS respondent maintained that this figure is suspect; he felt many of the immigrants may have gone through a QDE for assistance but then taken legalization applications themselves to the INS. He cautions that INS assessments can never be considered accurate.

Hal Ezell, western regional commissioner of the INS at the time IRCA was in force, emphasized that the legalization program required undocumented immigrants to trust the INS for the first time. To meet this challenge, a new bureaucracy had to be created in Los Angeles. The INS opened sixteen offices and hired a staff of twenty to twenty-five for each. According to respondents, the agency took advantage of the new staff to create a service-oriented atmosphere. For example, offices were set up in immigrant-friendly locations, such as malls and neighborhood centers. The INS also changed its first-come, first-serve practice, which had meant long lines and sometimes failure to serve some of its clients. During implementation of the legalization program, the INS mandated that its offices schedule client appointments to ensure better service.

Ernest Gustafson, the Los Angeles INS director, Hal Ezell, and a popular Spanish radio disc jockey known as El Tigre began a massive public relations campaign on television and radio and at community events throughout Los Angeles. The group called itself El Trio Amnestio. Ezell maintained that almost ten years after the media campaign he was still recognized by immigrants.

The Los Angeles district director of the INS at this time gave us one of the best examples of the agency's organizational environment and its effect on implementation:

> When amnesty really took off at the L.A. office, we had to hire a
> lot of extra people. Some were students, some were retired INS
> agents, and some were agents who were brought over from border
> patrol. We started to notice that the denial rate of aliens who were
> applying for amnesty was going up. We realized that it was because
> some of the same people who worked at keeping these people out
> were now asked to help them get rights. We immediately took
> them out of those positions.

The director felt that these types of problems occur quite often in the agency.

During the period when immigrants could apply for amnesty, the agency worked hard to change its image. The agency's outreach approach, however innovative, has not been used since. Commenting on his overall success, Ezell noted, "I just took the job with the idea that it could be done. Too many people now in the INS don't think this way. . . . I decided that there had never been a face associated with this agency until me." Recent sting and deportation operations, such as bringing undocumented immigrants into INS offices under false pretenses, have tarnished the positive image established during IRCA.

The director said that one of the most important nonstatutory objectives of legalization was to establish good rapport with the Spanish-speaking community. He recalled one occasion when a popular Spanish newscaster interviewed him and inquired about the benefits of legalization. The newscaster herself was not a legal immigrant. The director assisted the woman while ensuring confidentiality, emphasizing that by assisting her and other Spanish celebrities the INS began to establish a positive image in the immigrant community.

The INS found it difficult to estimate which types of ethnic groups would request legalization assistance. For example, Asian-Pacific leaders criticized the agency for failing to solicit Asian-Pacific applicants, claiming that too much attention was devoted to Latino immigrants (Baker-Gonzalez 1990). In Los Angeles, there were 120,000 to 150,000 undocumented immigrants of Asian-Pacific descent, of whom 36,000 to 75,000 would have been eligible for legalization (Baker-Gonzalez 1990).

In terms of residence and language, the Asian community is not as unified as the Latino community. Unlike the Latino community, the Asian-Pacific community is more widespread throughout the Los Angeles region. Further, unlike Latinos, the community does not share a language bond. For example, there are approximately fifteen Asian-Pacific countries represented in Los Angeles; however, there is not one major radio or television station. There is also no major religious or community organization like that of Latinos, although there is a strong affiliation with the Catholic Church (Rolph 1990).

The respondents felt that, unlike those of the sanctions program, the objectives of the legalization program were "real" and "tangible." For example, respondents felt that the legalization policy had a specific target group, a prescribed time frame for implementation, and a clearer set of goals. This clearly defined beginning-to-end phase was key to implementing legalization.

Despite clear overall objectives, INS representatives had difficulty interpreting some of the stipulations of legalization. For instance, the INS was not systematic in its interpretation of what constituted continuous residence and absence from the country. Some immigrants were told that the amount of time they spent outside the United States was acceptable, while others, sometimes from the same family, were penalized for exactly the same amount of time abroad (Alva, pers. com. 1990). The discretion afforded to INS representatives in implementing legalization prompted a tremendous number of legal challenges. Fifteen issues were eventually challenged in court, resulting in redefined deadlines and requirements. The issues included cases of departure, diplomatic and international visas, felony charges, HIV testing, reentry, and public charges (see Appendix 5).

In the end, federal courts held that the INS must interpret the requirements for the legalization provision more generously. An immigrant advocate commented on the multitude of legal challenges raised by MALDEF and the National Council of La Raza (NCLR): "It forced the agency to widen up the acceptance rate of immigrants applying for legalization." For instance, lawsuits ensued when the INS was unclear about what constituted "continuous residence" or "physical propensity." Some immigrants were accepted while others with the same qualifications were rejected. In this respondent's view, the number of legal challenges to legalization should be understood not as a failure but as a victory for immigrants who may otherwise have been left out of the legalization process.

Implementing Employer Sanctions

Respondents maintained continually that employers were to be carefully targeted and that strong pressure from those outside the agency, such as employer groups, mandated that the employment sector not be compromised when employing workers. This may or may not account for some of the implementation problems that occurred under the sanctions program.

When comparing the wording of the employer sanctions provision, most of the respondents felt that the objectives were not clear enough for INS enforcement. For example, one respondent maintained that in creating the INS guidelines for implementing sanctions in Los Angeles, it was not clear who was to be targeted for sanctions after the initial education campaign phase. If an employer took fraudulent work documentation, was the alien worker or the employer to be punished?

There was one legal challenge regarding clarity of wording. The case centered on the issue of defining the employer's obligation to ascertain the legal status of workers. The INS prevailed. Respondents maintained that because the INS wanted to ensure good rapport with the business community, they were careful not to disrupt relations, thereby avoiding litigation.

The INS was also significantly challenged in terms of targeting employers for sanctions. According to INS respondents, Los Angeles is distinguished by having many small and informal businesses. Because small businesses do not have formal chains of communication, they were not adequately informed about sanctions.

INS respondents felt that during the first two years of sanctions implementation, there was a slight decrease in the amount of immigration into the United States. Today undocumented immigration has probably exceeded rates prior to the passage of IRCA. Furthermore, as a result of sanctions, the fraudulent document industry has grown. Immigrants can purchase counterfeit Social Security cards as a way to circumvent sanctions. According to the INS respondents, these Social Security cards are so skillfully done that they cannot be detected as fraudulent. Moreover, they are quite easy to purchase. It is well known that fake cards can be purchased at any location in Los Angeles with a sign bearing the word "Micas." According to most respondents, unless a tamper-proof document is developed, sanctions will remain difficult to enforce. According to one INS respondent,

> If immigration is a problem, which according to the American people it is, sanctions must be made enforceable. Before this is possible the INS must first modify the single work authorization document and second, create a database for screening out aliens, because there is no computer database by which employers can verify documentation. Third, the agency must become more accessible to sanction questions. The INS is flooded with false documents. (Interview, 1998)

Respondents maintain that Americans are concerned about civil liberties and compare tamper-proof identification cards to those used in repressive countries. As one respondent told me, "If U.S. citizens really want to fix the immigration problem, which they say they do, then they've got to get over it" (interview, August 1999).

Sanctions is another example of an immigration policy characterized by contradictory objectives. For instance, one respondent maintained that employers are responsible for enforcing sanctions but have no way to screen fraudulent work authorization documents. Also, employers have to accept documentation at face value. Raids on employers can result in 30 to 40 percent of their workforce being deported, at no fault of the employers.

However, to complicate the issue, an attorney explained that employers themselves circumvent sanctions by encouraging the use of fraudulent documents. She has represented several clients whose employers have told their employees to purchase fraudulent documents. Employers themselves have called the INS to raid their own worksites, thereby avoiding the need to pay wages. Such actions are not penalized because the employer can claim that he or she examined the documentation. One attorney said, "Sometimes it's just easier hiring aliens and getting them fake documents than getting fined."

The GAO found that sanctions resulted in discriminatory practices against individuals who look foreign or have an accent. It also found that legal immigrants who were darker skinned or who had accents were less likely to be hired by employers and that the Los Angeles district is twice as likely to practice discrimination than are employers elsewhere. To date, Congress has not formally responded to these findings.

Most respondents felt that the sanctions program did not meet the goals set for it by IRCA. Today INS representatives confirm that the construction, garment, food, small manufacturing, light and house framing industries remain consistent offenders of sanctions in Los Angeles. Moreover, the increasing amount of undocumented immigration into the United States has further complicated enforcement. According to INS personnel, it is highly unlikely that there will ever be enough resources allocated to properly address this issue. Indicative of the shifts in popular sentiment, INS respondents also feel that sanctions have lost their political appeal to Congress. Patrolling the border has gained more importance than sanctions in terms of policy agendas.

Overall, the sanctions provision was most successful immediately after it was implemented. In 1988 studies by the GAO found that 85 percent of employers nationwide were aware of IRCA. Of those, a full 20 percent did not fully understand sanctions. A follow-up study in 1990 found that despite significant media and mailing campaigns and millions of direct employer contacts, only 60 percent of employers nationwide were aware of the sanctions provision, a reduction of 25 percent from the 1988 level (GAO 1991). Today approximately half of all employers are aware of sanctions.

Undocumented Immigration Today

Most respondents felt that legalization, rather than sanctions, was the great success of IRCA. The agency was able to change its image to one that was immigrant-safe, process a tremendous number of people, set up facilities in a short time, and foster trust. The number of individuals processed, approximately one million in Los Angeles alone, was an impressive accomplishment.

Legalization has had a tremendous impact. Immigrants whose status has changed from illegal to legal now have a sense of freedom, affecting how they look for work, buy a house, travel across the border, and visit relatives (Juffras 1991). Clearly, many people, approximately three million nationally, have benefited from the legalization program, and many of these immigrants have become naturalized citizens.

Overall, however, the Department of Justice found that adjudications were inconsistent, insufficiently documented, inadequately reviewed, and failed to comply with statutory requirements. As a result, legalization benefits may have been granted to ineligible applicants and denied to others who were eligible (U.S. Department of Justice 1989: 3).

Today it is clear just who the INS processed. Ninety-two percent of all legalization applicants in Los Angeles were Latino, 78 percent of whom were from Mexico. Legalization data also indicate that most applicants were male, eighteen to twenty-four years old, and had lived in the United States for approximately five years.

The Implications of IRCA Today

A review of how the INS is influenced by the immigration policy process is important for several reasons. This case study shows that IRCA was influenced by economic realities. Policy was written and implemented based on the economic needs of the time. Further, the importance of culture in the Latino community should not be underestimated. The INS had to craft policy to fit the special needs of the community in Los Angeles. The IRCA and INS case study in Los Angeles shows that given the right inducements, such as clear deadlines and high morale, the INS can be very good at implementing service policies rather than enforcement policies. This is important given the lower levels of funding afforded to service relative to enforcement.

The employer sanctions provision resulted in the escalation of the fraudulent document industry. The law did not set up a database that would allow business owners to check the validity of documentation. In general, sanctions are simply too difficult to enforce. The debate continues over whether Americans should possess a universal identification system and whether such a system could decrease undocumented immigration.

The INS respondents believe that the positive relationship developed with immigrant communities during IRCA has been destroyed. The shift in the public's attitudes encourages the INS to devote attention to patrolling the border and not to employer sanctions. This is unfortunate, because implementing sanctions is perhaps one of the more humane approaches to curbing immigration. A study conducted by the Center for Immigration Research found that an increase in border patrolling has coincided with an increase in the number of undocumented immigrant deaths. Since 1984 there have been 3,676 deaths related to illegal entries in areas not patrolled by the INS.

For immigrant advocates, the amnesty provision is perhaps the most beneficial piece of legislation for undocumented immigrants in the twentieth century. However, critics of amnesty maintain that immigrants are never punished for entering the country illegally, which tells undocumented immigrants that if they remain in the United States long enough another amnesty is inevitable.

Section 245(i) of the Immigration and Naturalization Act of 1998 allowed undocumented immigrants to apply for residency in the United States, providing they had sponsorship, from family or employers, and could pay a $1,000 penalty fee. The law expired in February 1998 but was reinstated for a few months by the Clinton administration in 2000. The INS has been overwhelmed with inquiries. Immigrants believe that 245(i) is the most recent version of amnesty. According to INS respondents, unscrupulous attorneys have been deceiving undocumented immigrants, charging them substantial fees to process their applications.

Finally, President Fox of Mexico as well as influential members of Congress believe that one way to decrease undocumented immigration is to establish another Bracero or Guest Worker Program. Critics of the Bracero Program contend that it exploited immigrants, affording them few rights. Furthermore, the Bracero Program increased rather than decreased undocumented immigration during the 1950s. Immigrants who no longer wished to work in the bracero system simply fled to other employers. Despite strong criticisms by immigrant advocates, a new bracero program is under consideration.

It appears that the immigration policy process is about to shift again. In an interview, Congressman Ed Pastor, formerly chair of the Hispanic Congressional Caucus, maintained that immigrant advocates have been pressuring for another amnesty if and when this new Bracero Program is implemented. An estimated 3 million to 4 million immigrants would apply for the new amnesty, a number similar to that before IRCA was enacted.

Chapter Five

Social Services

A CASE STUDY

IN THE 1990S POPULAR SENTIMENT led to the creation of the most controversial immigration legislation to date, California's Proposition 187, the Welfare Reform and Control Act, and the 1996 Immigration Reform Act. Their objective was to reduce immigration by denying social services, especially welfare, to both undocumented and legal immigrants. Welfare reform as an immigration deterrent became a policy agenda despite the fact that employment is the most significant reason for migrating to the United States.

This chapter shows that when enforcement policies were passed, the service side of the INS experienced a significant increase in workload. Characteristic of the immigration policy process, when welfare reforms were enacted, Mexican legal immigrants, fearful of losing benefits as a result of anti-immigrant sentiment, applied for naturalization in record numbers. The agency was not prepared for the significant rise in the number of applications from immigrants needing assistance. As a result, the quality of service afforded to Mexican immigrants suffered, and the INS appeared ineffective at carrying out its assigned mandates.

This case study illustrates that immigration policies are created with little understanding of the INS's capacity to carry them out. It also illustrates that these policies affect other, unrelated agencies.

Proposition 187

BACKGROUND

In the early 1990s public sentiment against undocumented as well as legal immigration resurfaced. On the assumption that the federal government had failed to control immigration, the momentum for immigration reforms grew. Border states, such as California, Texas, and Arizona, requested federal funding for more Border Patrol agents as a way to deter undocumented immigration. Some states sued the federal government for costs incurred by large undocumented populations. School systems with large undocumented communities complained that the federal government failed to subsidize adequately the costs of educating undocumented children. Federal moneys that were to be funneled back to states and local governmental agencies did not coincide with the growing needs of the undocumented community.

In the early 1980s many social programs, such as job training, energy and housing assistance, and legal services, that had been funded by the federal government were either cut or reassigned to the states. In the 1990s the impact of these cuts was devastating on poorer communities in states with large immigrant populations. Funding for some of these programs would now have to come out of the pockets of state residents. In short, the impact of 1980s federalism was taking its toll, further exacerbating relations between residents and immigrants.

Analysts contend that Proposition 187 may have been an unanticipated consequence of Proposition 13, an initiative passed in 1978 that limited property taxes in the state of California. Because state taxes and resources were reduced, redistributive expenditures, such as education, became more difficult to fund. As a result, immigrants were blamed for the economic downturn in the state.

Coinciding with anti-immigration sentiment was the gradual loss of jobs in the industrial sector and scarce state resources in large urban areas. In California, for instance, two hundred thousand defense-related jobs were lost as a result of the economic restructuring of the 1990s (Morales and Bonilla 1993). The Los Angeles Riots in 1992 exemplified the tension between newly arrived Latino immigrants and African Americans, caused by the loss of jobs. African Americans who had lived in the region for decades voiced frustration with Latino immigrants, blaming them for taking scarce jobs as well as for the economic downturn in the Los Angeles region (Pastor 1993).

PASSAGE

While unemployment grew, immigrants, especially the undocumented, became scapegoats for many of the economic problems in California. Residents approved Proposition 187, a highly controversial ballot initiative targeting undocumented immigrants in the state. According to this initiative, school districts and postsecondary schools were to stop providing educational services to undocumented students. School administrators would be required to verify the status of all newly admitted students by January 1, 1995, as well as the status of their parents. Students and parents unable to verify their status were to be reported to the INS and the California Attorney General. This initiative also prohibited all hospital administrators, both public and private, from providing nonemergency health care to the undocumented. Administrators of both health care and social services were required to report to the INS and the CAG undocumented immigrants who came to them seeking assistance.

In addition to eliminating basic social services, Proposition 187 established new criminal penalties for the manufacture or sale of false U.S. identification, such as Social Security cards and driver's licenses. Law enforcement agencies were also instructed to cooperate with the INS and the CAG in identifying and reporting undocumented persons living in California. Further, persons arrested by law enforcement agencies who were suspected of being undocumented would be required to verify their status.

ANALYSIS

After passage of Proposition 187, police officers, teachers, and social service workers, among many others, were responsible for reporting individuals who were undocumented to the INS. According to INS respondents, the resources necessary to respond to these newly appointed informers were astronomical.

Proposition 187 would also overturn previous Supreme Court decisions. In 1982 the Supreme Court had ruled in *Plyer v. Doe* that undocumented children should not be punished for the actions of their parents and that they have a constitutional right to education. The Court ruled further that immigration is a federal issue and should not be enforced by the states. Proposition 187 would shift the control of immigration to state and local jurisdiction. It would also turn teachers, social workers, and police officers into agents of the INS.

Criticisms regarding the feasibility of delegating yet more responsibilities to street-level bureaucrats ensued. In California, teachers' unions, numerous police associations, medical associations, and health administrators officially opposed the measure. In Los Angeles, the city council, the Board of Supervisors, and the Los Angeles Unified School District opposed the measure. One rationale for this opposition is that it is dangerous to assign local representatives the task of policing immigrants because it pushes undocumented immigrants deeper into a shadow society. For instance, if an undocumented woman were raped, would she feel comfortable asking for help from police or social workers who could report her illegal status to the INS?

The California Legislative Analyst Office, a nonpartisan arm of the California legislature, issued perhaps the most stinging analyses of Proposition 187. It found that passage would deprive the state of billions of federal dollars. For instance, fewer children in school would mean less federal funding. Already underfunded schools were not prepared for even more drastic cuts in their budgets. The analyses also showed that the consequences of denying medical services to undocumented immigrants would be increased costs for the state. For example, preventive care, such as testing for communicable diseases in the undocumented immigrant community, decreases long-term health care costs. Finally, there is not an accessible citizen database. Since U.S. citizens do not have a universal identification card, the notion that the INS or the CAG could identify and report undocumented persons living in California seemed impossible.

The Federation of Immigration Reform (FAIR) is a conservative group that advocates stricter immigration policies, such as reducing the overall number of immigrant admissions, as well as tightening penalties for immigrant violators. FAIR was perhaps the most vocal advocate of the initiative. Ironically, FAIR was made up of some of the same key players who implemented IRCA, which was designed to make the INS immigrant-friendly. For instance, Harold Ezell, western regional commissioner of the INS, and Alan Nelson, federal commissioner of the INS during IRCA, both advocated for Proposition 187. Proposition 187 would diminish any of the public relations gains made by the INS during IRCA. In an interview during the campaign for Proposition 187, Ezell explained the change in his attitude toward immigrants:

> I have never worked so hard in my life. The only thing we got is amnesty. Today, I would work just as hard to defeat it [IRCA] if it happened again. Three hundred thousand of these people who got amnesty are illiterate, never to become income producers. We have the displacement of people who are workers. It is not a race issue. I will never work on another amnesty [policy] again because I think it's bad for America. (Interview, 1994)

California Governor Pete Wilson used Proposition 187 in his platform for reelection. He attributed much of California's social service problems, such as overcrowding in schools and correctional facilities, to the presence of immigrants, both legal and undocumented. Wilson ran a television ad that contrasted pictures of immigrants taking their citizenship oaths with crowds of immigrants spilling over border areas. An announcer in the background said, "There is a right way and a wrong way to enter the country."

Because individuals who enter the United States illegally are barred from receiving welfare, Wilson's use of the welfare issue as a reason to vote for Proposition 187 was divisive and misguided at best. Two years before he came out in support of Proposition 187, Wilson called the conservative Patrick Buchanan and his attacks on undocumented immigrants racist. Even more intriguing, Wilson was a strong advocate for passage of IRCA, maintaining that it would be good for California's economy.

IMPACT

Proposition 187 passed by a two-to-one margin, with more than five million California voters voicing their support. Voter analyses indicate that many Californians were aware of the problems that would ensue after passage but wanted to use their votes to send a message to Washington that something needed be done to control undocumented immigration in the state (De Sipio and de la Garza 1998).

Nearly four out of five Latino voters opposed the proposition. Political analysts contend that Proposition 187 mobilized the Latino community and established important networks for working against future initiatives that were deemed "anti-Latino." In the years to follow, Latinos would mobilize again to oppose the eradication of bilingual education and affirmative action in California.

Proposition 187 was doomed from the start because states cannot control immigration. Immigration policies are enacted at the federal, not the state, level. An injunction was placed on the initiative immediately after passage. U.S. District Judge Mariana Pfaelzer declared Proposition 187 unconstitutional because it usurped the federal government's jurisdiction. Advocates of Proposition 187 challenged Judge Pfaelzer's decision, but the initiative was once again found unconstitutional. In July 1999 the final chapter of Proposition 187 played out. At the insistence of Governor Gray Davis, opponents of the proposition agreed to drop all future legal challenges.

The stipulation in Proposition 187 providing for greater collaboration between the INS and police agencies has been preserved in court. This means that in cities like Los Angeles, police officers may call the INS for assistance when they suspect a person is not a U.S. citizen or appears to be a non-U.S. citizen. An essential but overlooked consequence of this policy is the likelihood that this new relationship between police and the

INS deters undocumented immigrants from requesting police assistance. Crime victims may become hesitant to call the police, report crime, seek emergency assistance, and so on.

THE REACTION OF THE INS

The INS officially opposed Proposition 187 on the grounds that it was a poorly crafted policy. In a *Los Angeles Times* article on October 19, 1994, Doris Meissner stated that the initiative was flawed immigration policy and refused to support it. "We do not believe that the proposition is an effective way of enforcing the law against illegal aliens," she said. "The incentives for illegal immigrants are to work in the United States, not to sign up for welfare."

Respondents from the Los Angeles district office also said that they thought the policy was poorly formulated. One respondent explained, "We simply were not questioned as to how feasible it was going to be when we had to carry out the policy." Respondents feared passage of the proposition because the INS was already besieged with calls from the public about the status of suspected undocumented immigrants. This policy would only increase an already impossible workload. INS respondents also said that punishing children by denying education was a misguided and cruel way to control immigration. In general, Los Angeles INS respondents maintained that public attitudes resulted in poorly crafted policy.

Although Proposition 187 was never implemented, INS respondents in Los Angeles maintained that work on the service side tripled when large numbers of legal immigrants sought to protect themselves by becoming naturalized citizens. They described feeling overwhelmed by the significant boost in the number of immigrants wanting assistance.

Popular sentiment escalated around the issue of welfare use by immigrants. Welfare reform was gaining momentum at the federal level, and immigrants were growing more aware of possible changes in their benefits. Indicative of this fear of reform, the Western Region of the INS, made up of Alaska, Arizona, California, Hawaii, Nevada, Oregon, and Washington, experienced an overall increase of 120 percent in the number of immigrants wanting naturalization. Nationally, there was a nearly 80 percent increase in citizenship applications.

The Los Angeles INS district was feeling the brunt of this new shift in popular sentiment. On March 21, 1995, the *Los Angeles Times* interviewed Richard Rogers, Los Angeles INS district director. He maintained that the INS in Los Angeles experienced three times the amount of work processing naturalization requests. However, he attributed these requests to immigrants' desire to participate in electoral politics and not solely to welfare reform.

The policy director of NALEO maintained in an interview that during 1994–1995 she remembers seeing a significant increase in the number of elderly Latino immigrants seeking citizenship. Like Rogers, she attributed this increase to their wish to become eligible to vote. She recalled that one elderly woman wanted to become a U.S. citizen in order to vote against Pete Wilson, who had used immigrant bashing in his reelection campaign.

Welfare Reform and Immigrants at the National Level

Approximately one year after California voters passed Proposition 187, legal immigrants and welfare recipients became the targets at the federal level. With passage of the Personal Responsibility and Work Opportunity Reconciliation Act in 1996, Congress redefined who would be eligible for social services and how long a person could receive these benefits. In general, the law set a five-year ban on anyone using welfare. During their first five years in the United States, legal immigrants were to be denied SSI, food stamps, and AFDC. The law focused on legal immigrants because at no time were undocumented immigrants eligible for welfare.

Other legislation targeting immigrants and welfare was the Illegal Immigration Act of 1996. The law increased criminal penalties for immigration-related offenses, authorized increased enforcement personnel, and enhanced enforcement authority. It also provided for the hiring of more Border Patrol agents in subsequent years. Most important, the act imposed new requirements and restrictions on immigrant sponsors as well. It stipulated that if a family member sponsored an immigrant relative, he or she could not use any form of social services, such as welfare.

ANALYSIS OF WELFARE REFORM

Welfare reform had several unanticipated policy consequences. First, in many ways Congress motivated immigrants to apply for naturalization. Similar to the passage of Proposition 187, legal immigrants nationally were responding to anti-immigrant sentiment by ensuring their presence in the country and becoming U.S. citizens. Given the anti-immigrant sentiment during this period, it is not likely Congress wanted to increase the overall number of legal immigrants becoming U.S. citizens. On March 21,

1995, the *Los Angeles Times* ran the following article on the reaction of an elderly immigrant to welfare reform:

> Raul E. Dominguez immigrated from Cuba seven years ago, but only now has he applied for citizenship and enrolled in a class here to study the Constitution, the American Revolution and the abbreviations of the 50 states. Dominguez is doing so, at the tender age of 73, because Congress has threatened to cut off many federal benefits for legal immigrants.

There have been sad consequences of welfare reform. According to the Constitution, undocumented immigrants are entitled to emergency medical care. However, some immigrants, fearing deportation, will not request assistance. To accommodate their needs, a growing number of makeshift clinics have been set up where unlicensed individuals practice medicine in immigrant communities. In Los Angeles two children whose parents were afraid to take them to a reputable emergency care facility died after not receiving appropriate medical care.

Finally, Congress responded too quickly and too harshly when it came to targeting immigrant welfare users. Many of the cuts in welfare to immigrants were Social Security benefits allocated to the elderly. Congress miscalculated the public relations nightmare of denying senior citizens benefits. For instance, many constituents whose elderly parents were receiving Social Security benefits complained that the cuts were cruel and unfair. In an embarrassing move by Congress to appease angry constituents, in 1997 the decision to deny Social Security to elderly immigrants was rescinded. De Sipio and de la Garza maintain, "In relatively flush economic times, they [Congress] responded to pressure to restore social security benefits to legal immigrants."

THE REACTION OF THE INS TO WELFARE REFORM

The chief service officer of the Los Angeles INS district characterized politicians as "being unaware of agency performance while at the same time appearing tough on immigration." She maintained that there is a relationship between enforcement and service that is not fully understood by policy makers. She emphasized that when the initiative to restrict welfare and other social services began, politicians did not consider its potential effect on services.

According to INS respondents, the haste to adopt new immigration reform leaves insufficient time to put in place supplemental funding. Officials may receive orders to carry out a new mandate immediately, while the funds necessary to augment it are not allocated until the following year. In 1996, for instance, the district with the largest number of applicants for naturalization processing was Los Angeles. With a backlog of more than two hundred thousand applications, or one-fourth of all applications in the United States, it is not surprising that INS respondents continued to express feelings of being overwhelmed.

Indicative of the agency's bureaucratic rigidity as well as its poor communication style, respondents complained that it takes too long for organizational directives to be designed. One INS congressional researcher maintained that although the new laws passed in 1996, INS bureaucrats did not receive orders regarding how to implement them until May 1999. Immediately after the 1996 laws were passed, immigrants inundated the INS with requests for information. According to the researcher, agency representatives received requests for services they were unable to provide.

The assistant district director of detention and deportation in Los Angeles stated that the politics of immigration, especially undocumented immigration, are inconsistent. He went on to say that certain issues seem to hold more importance than others over time. Recent debates have focused on welfare and social services, whereas a decade ago the debate was limited primarily to employment, for example, employer sanctions.

NATURALIZATION THEORIES

In 1996 a new policy, known as "Citizenship USA," was implemented to speed up the naturalization process. A year after the policy was carried out, some members of Congress complained that the INS was naturalizing immigrants too quickly and not fully examining their cases. They charged that some immigrants were granted naturalization while others were being denied for the same reasons. Further, critics charged that those who were becoming citizens were likely to become Democrats, and therefore Citizenship USA was nothing more than an attempt to garner more constituents.

Investigations by the Department of Justice as to how the INS was implementing the policy ensued. In 1997 an audit found that there were a significant number of naturalized immigrants whose documentation was insufficient. For example, the study found that the Los Angeles district showed processing errors in 90.4 percent of its cases, and New York showed processing errors of 99 percent. Citizenship USA was eventually

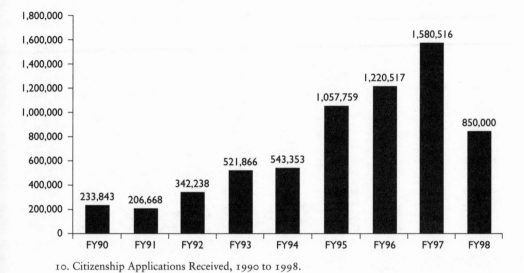

10. Citizenship Applications Received, 1990 to 1998.

halted. Several INS respondents pointed out that Congress criticized the INS for naturalizing immigrants too quickly whereas months earlier they were being criticized for not naturalizing immigrants quickly enough.

It should be noted that other factors, such as dual nationality, may contribute to the increased rate of naturalization. Between 1995 and 1998 the Mexican government was in the process of implementing dual nationality status to Mexican nationals living in the United States. Before this time, Mexican immigrants may not have sought U.S. citizenship because it would mean they would no longer be able to purchase property in Mexico.

Another explanation for the rise in citizenship applications is the green card replacement program. Respondents reported that they received complaints that the cost of new green cards was too high. Respondents believed that rather than pay for a new green card, immigrants would apply for citizenship.

Figures 10 through 13 were compiled from the *1998 INS Statistical Yearbook*. It is clear that citizenship rates went up overall in the previous decade, particularly from 1996 to 1998. The Los Angeles district administered the majority of citizenship oaths. Not surprisingly, Mexican immigrants made up the majority of applicants who were naturalized in 1996.

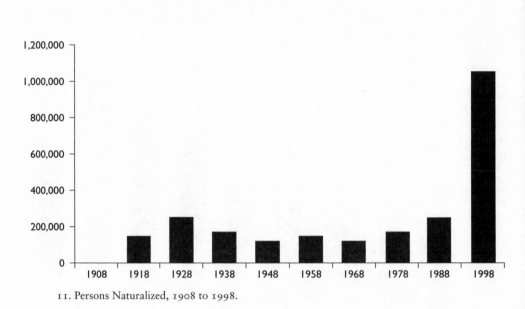

11. Persons Naturalized, 1908 to 1998.

Summary

This chapter underscores a variety of important themes of the immigration policy process. Immigration initiatives intended to be tough on immigration are formulated with little understanding of the immigration process. This points to the fact that the formulation of public policy is often guided more by public sentiment and less by reason. As a result, "get tough" policies that appeal to constituents' fears often result in the counterintuitive finding of increased naturalizations. Throughout the years in which Proposition 187 and the 1996 Welfare Reform Act have been in effect, we see corresponding increases in naturalizations.

Policies created for the enforcement side of the agency affect the quality of service that is afforded to immigrants on the other side of the agency. Welfare reforms, intended to be enforcement policies, have an impact on the service side. Recent efforts to decrease or deter immigration to the United States have in effect led to more immigrants seeking naturalization.

Politicians' use of negative stereotypes to appeal to constituents' fears has had a role in fostering punitive anti-immigrant legislation. The real social danger here is its deterrent effect on segments of our population who seek emergency medical and police aid. Out of fear of deportation and family separation, they may not get the assistance that they deserve.

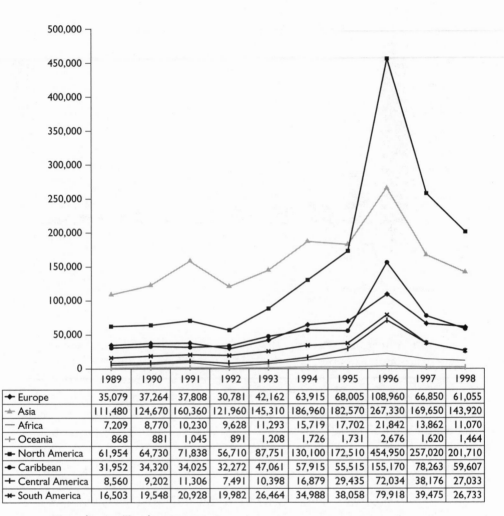

	1989	1990	1991	1992	1993	1994	1995	1996	1997	1998
◆ Europe	35,079	37,264	37,808	30,781	42,162	63,915	68,005	108,960	66,850	61,055
▲ Asia	111,480	124,670	160,360	121,960	145,310	186,960	182,570	267,330	169,650	143,920
— Africa	7,209	8,770	10,230	9,628	11,293	15,719	17,702	21,842	13,862	11,070
─┼─ Oceania	868	881	1,045	891	1,208	1,726	1,731	2,676	1,620	1,464
■ North America	61,954	64,730	71,838	56,710	87,751	130,100	172,510	454,950	257,020	201,710
● Caribbean	31,952	34,320	34,025	32,272	47,061	57,915	55,515	155,170	78,263	59,607
✛ Central America	8,560	9,202	11,306	7,491	10,398	16,879	29,435	72,034	38,176	27,033
✳ South America	16,503	19,548	20,928	19,982	26,464	34,988	38,058	79,918	39,475	26,733

12. Naturalization Trend, 1989 to 1998.

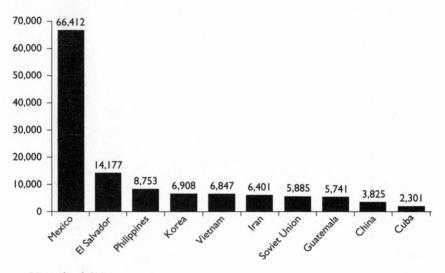

13. Naturalized Citizens, 1996.

Anti-immigrant sentiment that characterized the mid- to late 1990s served to mobilize politically the Latino population. In the years following Proposition 187, Latinos mobilized to fight the rollback of affirmative action and bilingual education. Some Latinos who became naturalized citizens as a result of anti-immigrant sentiment are now voting constituents. Newly released census data indicate that Latinos are the fastest-growing group in the country, and relations with undocumented immigrants have improved. On July 19, 1999, the *Los Angeles Times* reported:

> "The pendulum swung very far to the right; now it's swinging back to the middle," says Frank Sharry, executive director of the National Immigration Forum. "It's gone from being a race to the bottom to get tough on immigrants to who can be more pro-immigrant, without appearing to be soft on uncontrolled immigration."

Politicians will have to walk a fine line between being tough on immigration and not appearing to be anti-Latino, as immigration issues significantly affect the Latino community.

Chapter Six | *Where Are We in the Immigration Policy Process?*

The Immigration Policy Process

THIS STUDY EXAMINES the inside of the policy making and implementation cycles. It illustrates the crucial relationship among bureaucratic structures, laws, agency-level behavior, and the exploitation of Latino immigrants based on the prevailing political economy. The immigration policy process is influenced by a variety of forces—politics, popular sentiment, bureaucratic structures, and the economy, among others. Overall, immigration policies change the behaviors of street-level INS representatives. As a result, the quality of service afforded to Latino immigrants is poor. The INS is faced with having to implement a service versus sanction policy mandate that is limited by program budgets and the dramatic ebb and flow of public opinion. This research has implications for other agencies that are directed to carry out such mandates. It also points out that geographic location helps to either support or hinder implementation. This study would be color-blind if attention was not called to the fact that Latino immigrants continue to be exploited as a result of this policy process. Large segments of the U.S. population remain unwilling to examine the existing systematic biases against certain races and countries of origin.

It may be useful to summarize these dynamics. First, public opinion regarding immigration is influenced by a variety concerns, concerns that may be emotional or economic. Typically, these concerns emanate from the local political level and infiltrate state-level political discourse. The belief, for example, that there are too many immigrants taking American jobs or that immigrants are consuming an inordinate portion of available welfare resources eventually reaches the ears of politicians at the national level. Politicians, to appease constituents and mobilize votes, may create or recommend policies under the guise that they will decrease or deter immigration.

Public opinion favors the enactment of enforcement procedures such as increased border patrol and stricter penalties for undocumented immigration. Congress has been more active in enacting enforcement policies than service policies. The creation of federal immigration policies, according to respondents, only results in backlogs of work and inordinately complex objectives. Consequently, the quality of service on both the enforcement and the service side suffers. For instance, as a result of sting and deportation operations on the enforcement side, the organizational gains such as outreach and public relations on the service side diminish.

It is interesting to note that when immigration policies are formulated, particularly those directed at the undocumented, there is no established opposition on their behalf. Undocumented immigrants cannot vote. As a result, policies are enacted with little regard or concern for undocumented immigrants, which has resulted in discriminatory practices.

Unrealistic objectives characterized the case studies examined here. Unrealistic objectives are those that have no chance of being effective. For example, many respondents maintained that the employer sanctions provision was intentionally created to be unenforceable. In order for sanctions to work, INS respondents maintain, Congress would have to provide for a tamper-proof identification card. Rather than create policy that will actually be effective, respondents believe, it is easier for Congress to blame the INS for the amount of undocumented immigration into the United States. Other examples are policies that are passed under the guise of denying undocumented immigrants welfare. Even though welfare is not available to undocumented immigrants, politicians use welfare reform as a popular political agenda. Furthermore, policies that are distinguished by unrealistic objectives only serve to diminish the necessary support and commitment on the part of the INS to fulfill assigned duties.

Since immigration is a complicated phenomenon influenced by a variety of factors, INS representatives complained, the lack of insight on the part of politicians when writing laws only serves to complicate the agency's policy objectives. Immigration is an extremely complicated issue that is heavily influenced by partisan politics fueled by public opinion. When the INS is assigned new policy objectives, this is done with little consideration of its capacity to handle them. Agency performance is hampered by insufficient resources and an overwhelming number of responsibilities.

The dual mission of the agency is another characteristic of the immigration process. Undocumented immigrants have traditionally been fearful of the INS and therefore do not seek out the very agency responsible for helping them. This is important because respondents reported that policy makers do not take into account the influence that enforcement policies have on the service side of the agency. Stated simply, when enforcement policies are implemented—or in the case of Proposition 187, not being implemented—these policies appear to generate waves of immigrants who need assistance on the service side of the agency.

The cases of Proposition 187 and recent welfare reform illustrate that when policies were created to decrease immigration the effect was a hike in naturalization rates. INS representatives are well aware of this; politicians are not.

INS respondents maintained that when the agency is incapable of carrying out mandates, the tendency in Congress has been to change the agency's funding or create another policy directed at decreasing immigration. The agency is then left to grapple with these new conditions and is often seen as inadequate. Respondents stated that morale is low, that the public does not understand why the agency is not better able to carry out its mission, and that it continues to be responsible for contradictory mandates. They stated that their greatest satisfaction comes from implementing policies that are designed to assist immigrants.

The INS respondents on the service side believe that negative events, such as inadequate job performance and Border Patrol abuses, generate the most attention. Although respondents agree that there are problems within the agency, they maintain that a more careful examination would portray an INS that works very hard to enforce immigration laws. This suggests a need to examine how the dual mission of the agency influences immigrants as well as agency representatives.

My findings suggest that given the right policy design, the INS is more effective at implementing service policies than enforcement policies. Respondents attributed their success in implementing legalization to the clarity of the provision's objectives. They also stated that they enjoyed their role as advocates for the immigrant community. Both factors contributed to high morale among INS employees. My findings also suggest that the INS is more effective at servicing and eventually naturalizing immigrants who are already in the United States than at targeting them for deportation and other enforcement operations. Unfortunately, a smaller portion of the INS's budget is allocated to service activities than to enforcement activities.

Recommendations

Congress should reinstate a legalization policy such as that under IRCA, which led to a dramatic reduction in the need for policing operations. Furthermore, the reality is that some undocumented immigrants who enter the country are here to stay, regardless of their status. A legalization program is good social policy and effectively reduces the number of undocumented immigrants in the United States.

This has important implications for policy makers because the INS currently receives more resources from Congress to implement enforcement policies. Interviews conducted within the agency illustrate that the INS prefers the positive appeal of service policies, but enforcement policies tend to generate external support. One respondent explained that when the INS is called to testify before Congress, it sends a Border Patrol officer with a patrol dog. Although the Border Patrol receives only a part of the overall budget, the symbolic power of an agent with his dog generates support for INS efforts. In general, most of the respondents, INS representatives as well as immigrant advocates, felt service rather than enforcement policies are more successful.

A clear link between policy formation and the ability of the agency to fulfill its functions is required. Too many policies have been enacted with little consideration of their practicality or realistic chances of success.

Respondents believe that agency performance has suffered as a result of underfunding. Larger budgets should be granted to the agency, particularly to the service side. The quality of service can be improved by ensuring that assistance is provided in a shorter and more reasonable amount of time. More INS service representatives should be hired to answer on-site and telephone inquiries. Service delivery problems could also be resolved if a service attitude was rewarded. Also, by making it more difficult for employers to exploit workers and by ensuring higher wages and safer working conditions, all workers, citizens and undocumented immigrants alike, are protected. Instead of spending millions of dollars on employer sanctions, money should be directed toward enforcement of minimum wage laws and workplace safety laws.

Currently, the Bush administration advocates a change in the organization of the INS.

The Administration proposes restructuring and splitting the INS
into two agencies with separate chains of command and accounta-

bility, reporting to a single policy leader in the Department of Justice. One agency will be focused exclusively on service and the other will be focused exclusively on law enforcement. The Administration will work with Congress in a bipartisan manner to enact legislation that fundamentally improves the way the Nation's immigration system is administered. (Department of Justice 2001)

It is clear that the dual mission of the agency influences the immigration policy process. Separating the INS into two units would certainly eradicate problems that have been identified throughout this book. Congress should pursue separating the agency. However, respondents oppose this proposal because it will lead to new problems with which the INS will have to contend.

Based on the overall findings, the following organizational and policy incentives will improve the INS's quality of service. When the INS is delegated the task of implementing policy, it should clearly articulate objectives. Agency guidelines should include tangible directives, such as who is being targeted and specific time lines for implementation. IRCA illustrates the influence that federal, regional, and district directors and street-level bureaucrats can have on agency commitment. Policy players' awareness of schedules and deadlines and clear directives generate significant commitment on the part of policy players to meet desired objectives. In addition to having high-level involvement of policy managers, this scenario suggests that public support is an essential component for fostering agency commitment to policy objectives. These case studies demonstrate that implementation is more difficult in hostile environments. More resources allocated for public relations campaigns will lead to greater public support and, subsequently, facilitate agency commitment.

Policy actors must fit implementation schemes to the unique needs of communities. For instance, policy actors should consider local mediating structures, such as ethnic enclaves, religious organizations, and the media. The INS should offer services at sites in community settings, in addition to its offices. The INS achieved these goals when implementing IRCA.

Discretionary decisions and input rather than standardized organizational guidelines should characterize this implementation scenario, particularly when carrying out service policies. For example, INS representatives should be able to make quick decisions on applications without their supervisors' prior approval. Standardized application procedures exclude thousands of potential applicants. That is, as immigrants have varied and diverse histories, establishing flexible acceptance procedures on the part of the INS ensures that it will receive a more substantial and varied pool of applicants.

When asked how the quality of service could be improved, respondents maintained that assistance should be provided in a more reasonable amount of time. Applications should be processed more promptly, backlogged work should be completed, and questions should be answered on-site. Automated processing centers also need improvement. One respondent maintained, "We need a better identification system—we are investigating cases six years old."

New incentives for INS representatives to become more service oriented would improve both the quality of service and the public perception of the INS. Better bureaucratic organization would be a positive change for the agency and improve communication styles. Agency guidelines need to be clearly written and disseminated quickly.

Improving the working conditions of the INS seems daunting. How would improvements be developed and assessed? It is just not clear. On November 11, 1999, the *Washington Post* published an article on an INS director who attempted to change the environment of a district office to one that is more service friendly:

> Warren A. Lewis, the new head of the U.S. Immigration and Naturalization Service's Washington office, likes to refer to a statistic to describe his approach to the job: In only 18 months in office, he has reprimanded, suspended or otherwise disciplined more employees than his predecessors had in the last several years. As a result, he says, an office once saddled with a reputation for rude workers, long lines, inefficiency and even corruption has begun to provide better service to the hundreds of thousands of immigrants living in the District and Virginia who seek citizenship, green cards, work permits, visas or other benefits.

According to respondents, abuse of power is a problem on the enforcement side. Because abuses often go undetected, the agency needs to provide its employees with incentives to inform their supervisors when abuses occur. Respondents maintain that current working conditions sometimes dictate a "close-lipped" attitude.

Respondents also maintained that the enforcement mission of the agency weakens activities on the service side. It is imperative to carry out a campaign to educate the community as to both missions of the agency. This remains a challenge since many of the respondents on the enforcement side maintained that immigrants do not take their activities seriously.

More than half of all INS employees are Anglo, and more than one-fourth define themselves as Hispanic. Hispanic INS employees, however, are found predominantly in the Border Patrol. Therefore, Mexican immigrants are more likely to encounter Latino INS representatives when they are enforcing immigration law than when they are providing services. It would be beneficial to place more Latino INS representatives in the service sector. The assumption is that Hispanic employees are more sensitive to Mexican immigrant needs because they are familiar with the language and the culture. As of 2000, there were approximately 30,500 INS employees, 70 percent of whom are male. It is recommended that the INS hire more women. Female immigrants may feel better served by a representative who is of the same gender.

Predictions and the Immigration Policy Process

Job skills historically have not been a major consideration in determining the admissibility of immigrants because immigrants were easily absorbed into the unskilled labor sector. Today, this is not the case. As evidence, Microsoft's Bill Gates recently testified before Congress that he desperately needs workers for his company and that restrictions on high-skilled visa workers should be eased. The service sector is also in need of employees. Clearly, both high-skilled and low-skilled immigrant workers are important for the U.S. economy. For instance, the *Arizona Republic* published the following article on November 8, 1999:

> Faced with a dwindling number of workers to fill jobs as dishwashers, busboys, landscapers and maids, the Valley's hospitality industry is mining a new mother lode of employees: documented workers from countries as far away as Iran and the Sudan. Competition for legal workers is so fierce among hoteliers that the industry is raising wages, helping recruits learn English and running vans hundreds of miles a day from modest neighborhoods to fashionable resort cities where there are jobs but little or no low-income housing.

The 1998 Gallup Poll data suggest that a majority of Americans believe that most immigrants are undocumented and of Mexican descent. It is

reasonable to assume that this belief is attributable in large part to por-
trayals of immigration issues, particularly in the border states of the
Southwest. While there are legitimate immigration concerns, exaggerated,
misguided, and inflated accounts of immigrant issues by politicians perpetuate pejorative social stereotypes. The danger in perpetuating the ille-
gal-legal stereotype regarding Mexican immigration is that people can use
the distinction as a rationale to engage in racial discrimination without
threatening one's sense of egalitarianism. Examples of this effect in the
literature are many, though not with reference to Mexican Americans
particularly. For instance, the outward manifestation of prejudice may be
symbolic, as represented by voters rejecting public policy initiatives that
threaten the status quo (e.g., McConahay 1986; Sears 1988) or being less
likely to help minority individuals in emergency situations (e.g., Gaertner
and Dovidio 1977). In short, it is easier to vote for policies that are anti-
Latino because of already established negative stereotypes (Short and Magaña 2002).

However, the good news is that with waves of Latino immigrants becoming naturalized citizens and with the astounding growth of the Latino
population in the United States, politicians are giving greater attention to
these new constituents. The 2000 census shows that the Latino population increased by more than 35 percent in the 1990s. In the next decade,
it is predicted that Latinos will be the largest minority group in the nation. More important, Latinos vote and are no longer linked predominantly to one political party. Latinos are concentrated in five states: California, Texas, Florida, New York, and Illinois. On September 16, 1999,
the *Washington Post* illustrated the recent courting of Latinos by presidential candidates for the 2000 election:

> Gore's leading Republican rival, Texas Gov. George W. Bush,
> spent last night celebrating Mexican independence from Spain at
> a traditional Dieciseis de Septiembre (16th of September) party in
> Detroit. And over at the Republican National Committee, officials
> are finalizing plans to run the first-in-a-decade television ads tar-
> geting Latino voters. . . . Gore, who received a rousing welcome,
> bragged to the audience that his first grandchild was born on
> July 4. "My next one I hope will be born on Cinco de Mayo,"
> [he said].

Observers of the immigration policy process maintain that when the economy is relatively robust, businesses can hire more immigrant laborers

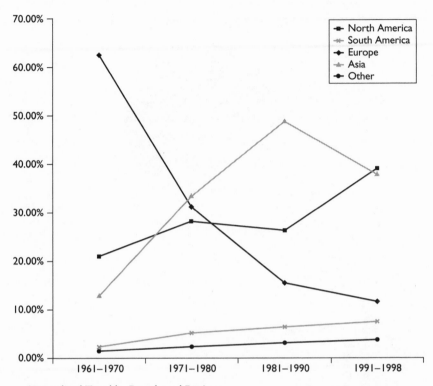

14. Naturalized Trend by Decade and Region.

without drawing the attention of those individuals who otherwise may perceive they are losing jobs or having social benefits drained. As evidence of this shift, businesses are requesting another Bracero Program to fill labor needs. Mexican laborers are provided temporary work permits by the United States for jobs in the service sector: the hospitality, agricultural, custodial, and gardening industries.

Simply put, when the economy is robust, immigration reform is given less attention by policy makers. When he was still Texas governor, George Bush used state money to assist elderly and disabled immigrants who no longer could use federal food stamps, and then-Vice President Al Gore announced plans to restore another $1.3 billion in food, disability, and health care benefits to legal immigrants. There was virtually no debate about allocating these funds back to immigrant communities.

The INS will continue to have a profound influence on the lives of Mexican immigrants, both legal and undocumented. (See Figures 14 through 17.) This prediction is based on a variety of sources and previous demo-

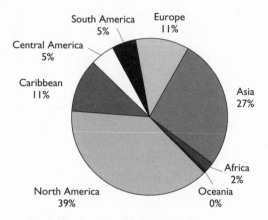

15. Naturalization Distribution, 1998.

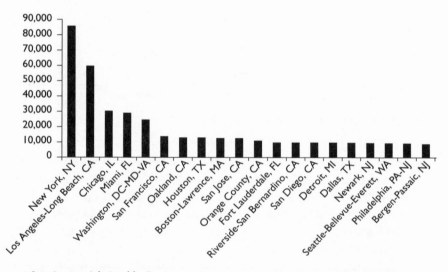

16. Immigrants Admitted by Region, 1998.

graphic trends. First, naturalization rates for individuals from North America have consistently risen since 1965. Not surprisingly, Mexican immigrants are the largest group to apply for naturalization. Large cities, such as New York and Los Angeles, will continue to be points of entry for immigrants. Second, Mexican immigrants will continue to be the largest immigrant group legally admitted to the United States.

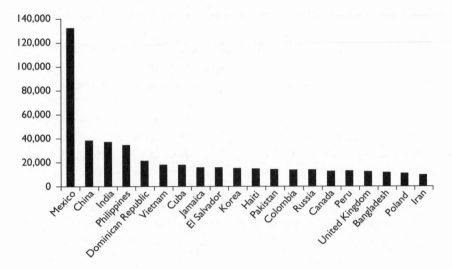

17. Immigrants Admitted by Country, 1998.

Third, the September 11 attacks on the World Trade Center and the Pentagon resulted in dramatic new policy mandates for the INS to implement. Indicative of the reactive nature of immigration policy, immediately after the attacks, the INS was charged with sealing off the nation's borders and deploying INS agents to airports. The process of deployment was cumbersome because Border Patrol agents are directed by sector chiefs who are under the supervision of regional directors who then report to the national director. Because of the difficulty of getting resources and manpower to sites expeditiously in the event of an emergency, the chief Border Patrol person will now have direct authority over the twenty-one Border Patrol sectors.

As a result of the attacks, popular sentiment shifted from illegal immigration to visa overstayers, that is, immigrants who remained in the country after their visas expired. Because several of the terrorists had entered the United States "legally," the public demanded to know how this could happen. The INS was viewed as inept. Politicians, quick to respond, set the stage for a variety of funding initiatives to resolve the problem of visa overstayers. Although INS representatives had complained about the problem well before the attacks, a new system for reporting the status of foreign and exchange students is being implemented. Another recommendation as a result of September 11 is that the agency would be taken from the jurisdiction of the Justice Department and placed under the newly created Department of Homeland Security. President Bush advocates placing the agency in the department as better preparation in the event of future attacks. It remains to be seen if these moves will improve the overall performance of the agency. The INS has been moved from one federal department to another many times, yet the organizational problems have remained unresolved.

Immigration to the United States, both legal and undocumented, is complex. If my findings show anything, it is that the INS does not implement policy in isolation. Rather, it is responsible for multifaceted and sometimes illogical tasks. The agency is accountable to a variety of interests that are constantly changing—popular sentiment, the economy, Congress, and the business sector, to name but a few. Because carrying out immigration policy is complicated, the INS will continue to straddle a variety of immigration interests, never truly appearing effective as an agency.

Appendix One

Immigration Reform and Control Act of November 6, 1986

(100 STATUTES-AT-LARGE 3359)

Comprehensive immigration legislation:

a. Authorized legalization (i.e., temporary and then permanent resident status) for aliens who had resided in the United States in an unlawful status since January 1, 1982 (entering illegally or as temporary visitors with authorized stay expiring before that date or with the Government's knowledge of their unlawful status before that date) and are not excludable.

b. Created sanctions prohibiting employers from knowingly hiring, recruiting, or referring for a fee aliens not authorized to work in the United States.

c. Increased enforcement at U.S. borders.

d. Created a new classification of seasonal agricultural worker and provisions for the legalization of certain such workers.

e. Extended the registry date (i.e., the date from which an alien has resided illegally and continuously in the United States and thus qualifies for adjustment to permanent resident status) from June 30, 1948, to January 1, 1972.

f. Authorized adjustment to permanent resident status for Cubans and Haitians who entered the United States without inspection and had continuously resided in the country since January 1, 1982.

g. Increased the numerical limitation for immigrants admitted under the preference system for dependent areas from 600 to 5,000 beginning in fiscal year 1988.

h. Created a new special immigrant category for certain retired employees of international organizations and their families and a new nonimmigrant status for parents and children of such immigrants.

i. Created a nonimmigrant Visa Waiver Pilot program allowing certain aliens to visit the United States without applying for a nonimmigrant visa.

j. Allocated 5,000 nonpreference visas in each of fiscal years 1987 and 1988 for aliens born in countries from which immigration was adversely affected by the 1965 act.

Appendix Two

Text of Proposition 187

Proposed Law

Section 1. Findings and Declaration.

The People of California find and declare as follows: That they have suffered and are suffering economic hardship caused by the presence of illegal aliens in this state. That they have suffered and are suffering personal injury and damage caused by the criminal conduct of illegal aliens in this state.

That they have a right to the protection of their government from any person or persons entering this country unlawfully. Therefore, the People of California declare their intention to provide for cooperation between their agencies of state and local government with the federal government, and to establish a system of required notification by and between such agencies to prevent illegal aliens in the United States from receiving benefits or public services in the State of California.

Section 2. Manufacture, Distribution or Sale of False Citizenship or Resident Alien Documents: Crime and Punishment. Section 113 is added to the Penal Code, to read:

113. Any person who manufactures, distributes or sells false documents to conceal the true citizenship or resident alien status of another person is guilty of a felony, and shall be punished by imprisonment in the state prison for five years or by a fine of seventy-five thousand dollars ($75,000).

Section 3. Use of False Citizenship or Resident Alien Documents: Crime and Punishment.

Section 114 is added to the Penal Code, to read:

114. Any person who uses false documents to conceal his or her true citizenship or resident alien status is guilty of a felony, and shall be punished by imprisonment in the state prison for five years or by a fine of twenty-five thousand dollars ($25,000).

Section 4. Law Enforcement Cooperation with INS. *Section 834b is added to the Penal Code, to read:*

834b. (a) Every law enforcement agency in California shall fully cooperate with the United States Immigration and Naturalization Service regarding any person who is arrested if he or she is suspected of being present in the United States in violation of federal immigration laws.

(b) With respect to any such person who is arrested, and suspected of being present in the United States in violation of federal immigration laws, every law enforcement agency shall do the following:

(1) Attempt to verify the legal status of such person as a citizen of the United States, an alien lawfully admitted as a permanent resident, an alien lawfully admitted for a temporary period of time or as an alien who is present in the United States in violation of immigration laws. The verification process may include, but shall not be limited to, questioning the person regarding his or her date and place of birth, and entry into the United States, and demanding documentation to indicate his or her legal status.

(2) Notify the person of his or her apparent status as an alien who is present in the United States in violation of federal immigration laws and inform him or her that, apart from any criminal justice proceedings, he or she must either obtain legal status or leave the United States.

(3) Notify the Attorney General of California and the United States Immigration and Naturalization Service of the apparent illegal status and provide any additional information that may be requested by any other public entity.

(c) Any legislative, administrative, or other action by a city, county, or other legally authorized local governmental entity with jurisdictional boundaries, or by a law enforcement agency, to prevent or limit the cooperation required by subdivision (a) is expressly prohibited.

Section 5. Exclusion of Illegal Aliens from Public Social Services.

Section 10001.5 is added to the Welfare and Institutions Code, to read:

10001.5. (a) In order to carry out the intention of the People of California that only citizens of the United States and aliens lawfully admitted to the United States may receive the benefits of public social services and to ensure that all persons employed in the providing of those services shall diligently protect public funds from misuse, the provisions of this section are adopted.

(b) A person shall not receive any public social services to which he or she may be otherwise entitled until the legal status of that person has been verified as one of the following:

(1) A citizen of the United States.

(2) An alien lawfully admitted as a permanent resident.

(3) An alien lawfully admitted for a temporary period of time.

(c) If any public entity in this state to whom a person has applied for public social services determines or reasonably suspects, based upon the information provided to it, that the person is an alien in the United States in violation of federal law, the following procedures shall be followed by the public entity:

(1) The entity shall not provide the person with benefits or services.

(2) The entity shall, in writing, notify the person of his or her apparent illegal immigration status, and that the person must either obtain legal status or leave the United States.

(3) The entity shall also notify the State Director of Social Services, the Attorney General of California, and the United States Immigration and Naturalization Service of the apparent illegal status, and shall provide any additional information that may be requested by any other public entity.

Section 6. Exclusion of Illegal Aliens from Publicly-Funded Health Care.
Chapter 1.3 (commencing with Section 130) is added to Part 1 of Division 1 of the Health and Safety Code, to read: Chapter 1.3. Publicly Funded Health Care Services 130.

(a) In order to carry out the intention of the People of California that, excepting emergency medical care as required by federal law, only citizens of the United States and aliens lawfully admitted to the United States may receive the benefits of publicly-funded health care, and to ensure that all persons employed in the providing of those services shall diligently protect public funds from misuse, the provisions of this section are adopted.

(b) A person shall not receive any health care services from a publicly-funded health care facility, to which he or she is otherwise entitled until the legal status of that person has been verified as one of the following: (1) A citizen of the United States. (2) An alien lawfully admitted as a permanent resident. (3) An alien lawfully admitted for a temporary period of time.

(c) If any publicly funded health care facility in this state from whom a person seeks health care services, other than emergency medical care as required by federal law, determines or reasonably suspects, based upon the information provided to it, that the person is an alien in the United States in violation of federal law, the following procedures shall be followed by the facility: (1) The facility shall not provide the person with services. (2) The facility shall, in writing, notify the person of his or her apparent illegal immigration status, and that the person must either obtain legal status or leave the United States. (3) The facility shall also notify the State Director of Health Services, the Attorney General of California, and the United States Immigration and Naturalization Service of the apparent illegal status, and shall provide any additional information that may be requested by any other public entity.

(d) For purposes of this section "publicly-funded health care facility" shall be defined as specified in Sections 1200 and 1250 of this code as of January 1, 1993.

Section 7. Exclusion of Illegal Aliens from Public Elementary and Secondary Schools.

Section 48215 is added to the Education Code, to read: 48215.

(a) No public elementary or secondary school shall admit, or permit the attendance of, any child who is not a citizen of the United States, an alien lawfully admitted as a permanent resident, or a person who is otherwise authorized under federal law to be present in the United States.

(b) Commencing January 1, 1995, each school district shall verify the legal status of each child enrolling in the school district for the first time in order to ensure the enrollment or attendance only of citizens, aliens lawfully admitted as permanent residents, or persons who are otherwise authorized to be present in the United States.

(c) By January 1, 1996, each school district shall have verified the legal status of each child already enrolled and in attendance in the school district in order to ensure the enrollment or attendance only of citizens, aliens lawfully admitted as permanent residents, or persons who are otherwise authorized under federal law to be present in the United States.

(d) By January 1, 1996, each school district shall also have verified the legal status of each parent or guardian of each child referred to in subdivisions (b) and (c), to determine whether such parent or guardian is one of the following: (1) A citizen of the United States. (2) An alien lawfully admitted as a permanent resident. (3) An alien admitted lawfully for a temporary period of time.

(e) Each school district shall provide information to the State Superintendent of Public Instruction, the Attorney General of California, and the United States Immigration and Naturalization Service regarding any enrollee or pupil, or parent or guardian, attending a public elementary or secondary school in the school district determined or reasonably suspected to be in violation of federal immigration laws within forty-five days after becoming aware of an apparent violation. The notice shall also be provided to the parent or legal guardian of the enrollee or pupil, and shall state that an existing pupil may not continue to attend the school after ninety calendar days from the date of the notice, unless legal status is established.

(f) For each child who cannot establish legal status in the United States, each school district shall continue to provide education for a period of ninety days from the date of the notice. Such ninety day period shall be utilized to accomplish an orderly transition to a school in the child's country of origin. Each school district shall fully cooperate in this transition effort to ensure that the educational needs of the child are best served for that period of time.

Section 8. Exclusion of Illegal Aliens from Public Postsecondary Educational Institutions.

Section 66010.8 is added to the Education Code, to read: 66010.8. (a) No public institution of postsecondary education shall admit, enroll, or permit the attendance of any person who is not a citizen of the United States, an alien lawfully admitted as a permanent resident in the United States, or a person who is otherwise authorized under federal law to be present in the United States.

(b) Commencing with the first term or semester that begins after January 1, 1995, and at the commencement of each term or semester thereafter, each public postsecondary educational institution shall verify the status of each person enrolled or in attendance at that institution in order to ensure the enrollment or attendance only of United States citizens, aliens lawfully admitted as permanent residents in the United States, and persons who are otherwise authorized under federal law to be present in the United States.

(c) No later than 45 days after the admissions officer of a public postsecondary educational institution becomes aware of the application, enrollment, or attendance of a person determined to be, or who is under reasonable suspicion of being, in the United States in violation of federal immigration laws, that officer shall provide that information to the State Superintendent of Public Instruction, the Attorney General of California, and the United States Immigration and Naturalization Service. The information shall also be provided to the applicant, enrollee, or person admitted.

Section 9. Attorney General Cooperation with the INS.

Section 53069.65 is added to the Government Code, to read: 53069.65. Whenever the state or a city, or a county, or any other legally authorized local governmental entity with jurisdictional boundaries reports the presence of a person who is suspected of being present in the United States in violation of federal immigration laws to the Attorney General of California, that report shall be transmitted to the United States Immigration and Naturalization Service. The Attorney General shall be responsible for maintaining on-going and accurate records of such reports, and shall provide any additional information that may be requested by any other government entity.

Section 10. Amendment and Severability.

The statutory provisions contained in this measure may not be amended by the Legislature except to further its purposes by statute passed in each house by rollcall vote entered in the journal, two-thirds of the membership concurring, or by a statute that becomes effective only when approved by the voters. In the event that any portion of this act or the application thereof to any person or circumstance is held invalid, that invalidity shall not affect any other provision or application of the act, which can be given effect without the invalid provision or application, and to that end the provisions of this act are severable.

Information taken from the California Secretary of State's Office 1994 General Election.

Appendix Three

Personal Responsibility and Work Opportunity Reconciliation Act of August 22, 1996

(110 STATUTES-AT-LARGE 2105)

Provisions: a. Established restrictions on the eligibility of legal immigrants for means-tested public assistance:

1. Barred legal immigrants (with certain exceptions) from obtaining food stamps and Supplemental Security Income (SSI) and established screening procedures for current recipients of these programs;

2. Barred legal immigrants (with certain exceptions) entering the U.S. after date of enactment from most federal means-tested programs for 5 years;

3. Provided states with broad flexibility in setting public benefit eligibility rules for legal immigrants by allowing states to bar current legal immigrants from both major federal programs and state programs;

4. Increased the responsibility of the immigrants' sponsors by making the affidavit of support legally enforceable, imposing new requirements on sponsors, and expanding sponsor-deeming requirements to more programs and lengthening the deeming period.

5. Broadened the restrictions on public benefits for illegal aliens and non-immigrants. a. Barred illegal, or "not qualified aliens," from most federal, state and local public benefits. b. Required INS to verify immigration status in order for aliens to receive most federal public benefits.

Appendix Four

Illegal Immigration Reform and Immigrant Responsibility Act of September 30, 1996

(110 STATUTES-AT-LARGE 3009)

Provisions: a. Established measures to control U.S. borders, protect legal workers through worksite enforcement, and remove criminal and other deportable aliens:

1. Increased border personnel, equipment, and technology as well as enforcement personnel at land and air ports of entry;

2. Authorized improvements in barriers along the Southwest border;

3. Increased anti-smuggling authority and penalties for alien smuggling;

4. Increased penalties for illegal entry, passport and visa fraud, and failure to depart;

5. Increased INS investigators for worksite enforcement, alien smuggling, and visa overstayers;

6. Established three voluntary pilot programs to confirm the employment eligibility of workers and reduced the number and types of documents that may be presented to employers for identity and eligibility to work;

7. Broadly reformed exclusion and deportation procedures, including consolidation into a single removal process as well as the institution of expedited removal to speed deportation and alien exclusion through more stringent grounds of admissibility;

8. Increased detention space for criminal and other deportable aliens;

9. Instituted 3-and 10-year bars to admissibility for aliens seeking to reenter after having been unlawfully present in the United States;

10. Barred re-entry of individuals who renounced their U.S. citizenship in order to avoid U.S. tax obligations.

b. Placed added restrictions on benefits for aliens:

1. Provided for a pilot program on limiting issuance of driver's licenses to illegal aliens;

2. Declared aliens not lawfully present ineligible for Social Security benefits;

3. Established procedures for requiring proof of citizenship for Federal public benefits;

4. Established limitations on eligibility for preferential treatment of aliens not lawfully present on the basis of residence for higher education benefits;

5. Provided for verification of immigration status for purposes of Social Security and higher educational assistance;

6. Tightened the requirement for an affidavit of support for sponsored immigrants, making the affidavit a legally binding contract to provide financial support;

7. Provided authority of States and political subdivisions of States to limit assistance to aliens in providing general cash public assistance;

8. Increased maximum criminal penalties for forging or counterfeiting the seal of a Federal department or agency to facilitate benefit fraud by an unlawful alien.

c. Miscellaneous provisions:

1. Recodified existing INS regulations regarding asylum;

2. Provided that the Attorney General's parole authority may be exercised only on a case-by-case basis for urgent humanitarian reasons or significant public health.

3. Created new limits on the ability of F-1 students to attend public schools without reimbursing those institutions;

4. Established new mandates for educational institutions to collect information on foreign students' status and nationality and provide it to INS;

5. Tightened restrictions regarding foreign physicians' ability to work in the United States;

6. Added new consular processing provisions and revised the visa waiver program.

Appendix Five | *Policy Summary*

ISSUES	REGULATORY ISSUES
Texas DWI cases except despite felony classification.	This cleared confusion in terms of when DWI is considered a felony; without this change, persons in other states would have been eligible while Texans would not because of differences in law.
Departure from United States does not interrupt continuous residency requirement.	Partially clarified what kinds of departures would violate the continuous residency requirement.
Foreign students with duration of status (D/S) eligible if study completed before 1/1/82.	Clarified at what point students had overstayed their visas "illegally in the U.S."; legalization required that the applicant have illegal status before 1/1/82.
Waivers—clarification of humanitarian, family unity, public interest grounds	The status allowed waivers for humanitarian, family unity, and public interest reasons; some definition of these terms provided by the INS.
HIV testing	Announcement of requirements as of 12/1/87. In separate legislation, Congress mandated that aliens be tested for HIV. This clarified the requirement for legislation applicants.
Asylum applicants	Eligible if filed before 1/1/82. Clarified the eligibility of asylum applicants by virtue of petition for

	asylum, could have been considered something other than "illegal" immigrants, thus making them ineligible to legalize.
Felony	Treated as misdemeanor where states so defines and sentence is less than 1 year (resolves #1 above). Further clarified the difference between a felony and misdemeanor.
Public charge	Clarifies standards for public cash assistance. Provided some clarification of what factors would be considered in determining whether an applicant was "likely to become a public charge."
Reentry—eligibility for unlawful nonimmigrants who entered United States with valid visa.	This affected undocumented immigrants who left the United States and returned on visitors' or other visas. Such visas were considered fraudulent because the traveler was a resident, not a visitor. This ruling determined that leaving the country did not jeopardize the applicant's eligibility.
Foster care—considered public cash assistance but not sole determinant of public charge.	This clarified whether being a foster child receiving aid or being a foster parent made an applicant ineligible. Funds for foster parents were deemed "cash assistance," for the purposes of determining whether the applicant was likely to become a public charge.
HIV testing—instruction to physicians	Further clarified the new HIV test requirement.
Interim rule—publication	Codified changes in regulations incorporating policy changes above.

SOURCE: From Cecilia Muñoz, "Unfinished Business: The Immigration Reform and Control Act of 1986."

Appendix Six | *Protocol Questions*

What is your title?

What are your responsibilities and duties?

Would you prefer your name and identity to be anonymous in this research?

Could you explain your particular role with regard to immigration policies?

What is your impression of the immigration policy process?

How would you briefly describe the INS's organizational agenda?

What do you consider INS's main objectives?

What organizational characteristic affects the implementation process of immigration policy?

Do you think the INS is better able to implement enforcement style (Sanctions) or service style (Legalization) immigration policies? Why?

What should be the first priority of an INS employee when implementing immigration policy?

What do you think is the perception of your agency on the part of the undocumented? the public? the government? If you wanted to, how would you change it?

Do you think INS employees are compensated adequately in comparison to other agencies?

Do you think INS agents have enough discretion when they make decisions regarding immigration policy at the street level?

If you could *not* base your opinion on statistics, how would you measure a successful immigration policy?

What do you consider to be the biggest obstacle when implementing immigration policy?

On a scale of 1-2-3-4-5, what would you rate the overall immigration policy process as it applies to the INS?

Appendix Seven

Immigration Laws, 1790–1996

Act of 1790

First federal act that established a uniform rule for naturalization by setting the resident requirement at two years.

Act of 1795

Repealed the 1790 act, increased the residence requirement to five years, and required a declaration of intention to seek citizenship at least three years before naturalization.

Naturalization Act of 1798

Provided that clerks of court must furnish information about each record of naturalization to the secretary of state, required registry of each alien residing in the United States, and increased the resident requirement for naturalization to fourteen years.

Aliens Act of 1798

The first federal law pertinent to immigration rather than naturalization. Authorized the president to arrest and/or deport aliens, and required the captain of any vessel to report the arrival of aliens on board. This law expired two years after it was enacted.

Alien Enemy Act of 1798

Provided that in the case of declared war or invasion the president shall have the power to restrain or remove alien enemy males of fourteen years and up but with due protection of their property rights as stipulated by treaty.

Naturalization Act of 1802

Reduced the residence requirement for naturalization from fourteen to five years. Established basic requirements for naturalization, including good moral character, allegiance to the Constitution, a formal declaration of intention, and witnesses.

Steerage Act of 1819

Established the continuing reporting of immigration to the United States by requiring that passenger lists or manifests of all arriving vessels be delivered to the local collector of customs, with copies transmitted to the secretary of state and the information reported to Congress.

Act of 1824

Facilitated the naturalization of aliens who had entered the United States as minors, by setting a two-year instead of a three-year interval between declaration of intention and admission to citizenship.

Act of 1847

"Passenger Acts," provided specific regulations to safeguard passengers on merchant vessels.

Passenger Act of 1855

Reaffirmed the duty of the captain of any vessel to report the arrival of alien passengers. Established separate reporting to the secretary of state distinguishing between permanent and temporary immigration.

Act of 1862

Prohibited the transportation of Chinese "coolies" on American vessels.

Act of 1864

Provided for the appointment of a commissioner of immigration by the president to serve under the authority of the secretary of state. Authorized immigrant labor contracts whereby would-be immigrants would pledge their wages to pay for transportation. Repealed in 1868.

Naturalization Act of 1870

Established a system of controls on the naturalization process and penalties for fraudulent practices. Extended the naturalization laws to aliens of African nativity and to persons of African descent.

Act of 1875

Established the policy of direct federal regulation of immigration by prohibiting entry to undesirable immigrants for the first time. Excluded criminals and prostitutes from admission. Prohibited the bringing of any Oriental persons without their free and voluntary consent, and declared the contracting of "coolie" labor a felony.

Chinese Exclusion Act of 1882

Suspended immigration of Chinese laborers to the United States for ten years. Repealed in 1943.

Immigration Act of 1882

Broadened restrictions on immigration by adding to the classes of inadmissible aliens, including persons likely to become public charges. Introduced a tax of 50 cents on each passenger brought to the United States.

Act of 1885

The first "Contract Labor Law." Made it unlawful to import aliens into the United States under contract for the performance of labor or services of any kind.

Act of February 1887

Amended the Contract Labor Law to render it enforceable by charging the secretary of the treasury with enforcement of the act and providing that prohibited persons be sent back on arrival.

Act of March 1887

Restricted the ownership of real estate in the United States to American citizens and those who had lawfully declared their intentions to become citizens, with certain exceptions.

Act of 1888

First measure since the Aliens Act of 1798 to provide for expulsion of aliens. Directed the return within one year after entry of any immigrant who had landed in violation of the Contract Labor Laws.

Immigration Act of 1891

Established the Bureau of Immigration under the Department of the Treasury to administer all immigration laws. Further restricted immigration by adding to the inadmissible classes persons likely to become public charges. Directed the deportation of any alien who entered the United States unlawfully.

Act of 1893

Added to the reporting requirements for alien arrivals to the United States information on occupation, marital status, ability to read or write, amount of money in possession, and physical and mental health.

Act of 1902

Extended the existing Chinese Exclusion Acts until such time as a new treaty with China was negotiated and extended the application of the exclusion acts to insular territories of the United States, including the requirement of a certificate of residence, except in Hawaii.

Act of 1903

Transferred the Bureau of Immigration to the newly created Department of Commerce and Labor and expanded the authority of the commissioner-general of immigration in the areas of rule making and enforcement of immigration laws.

Immigration Act of 1903

Added to the list of inadmissible immigrants. First measure to provide for the exclusion of aliens on the grounds of proscribed opinions by excluding "anarchists." Provided for the deportation of aliens who became public charges within two years after entry from causes existing prior to their landing.

Act of 1904

Reaffirmed and made the permanent the Chinese exclusion laws. In addition, clarified the territories from which Chinese were to be excluded.

Naturalization Act of 1906

Combined the immigration and naturalization functions of the federal government, changing the Bureau of Immigration to the Bureau of Immigration and Naturalization. Established fundamental procedural safeguards regarding naturalization, such as fixed fees and uniform naturalization forms. Made knowledge of the English language a requirement for naturalization.

Immigration Act of 1907

Required aliens to declare intention of permanent or temporary stay in the United States and officially classified arriving aliens as immigrants and non-immigrants. Increased the head tax to $4. Added to the excludable classes imbeciles, feeble-minded persons, and persons with mental defects.

White Slave Traffic Act of 1910

Also known as the Mann Act. Prohibited the importation of women via interstate transportation for immoral purposes.

Act of 1913

Divided the Department of Commerce and Labor into separate departments and transferred the Bureau of Immigration and Naturalization to the Department of Labor. It further divided the Bureau of Immigration and Naturalization into a separate Bureau of Immigration and Bureau of Naturalization, each headed by its own commissioner.

Immigration Act of 1917

Excluded illiterate aliens from entry. Expanded the list of aliens excluded for mental health and other reasons. Further restricted the immigration of Asian persons, creating the "barred zone" (known as the Asian-Pacific triangle), natives of which were declared inadmissible.

Act of 1918

Known as the "Entry and Departure Controls Act." Authorized the president to control the departure and entry in times of war or national emergency of any alien whose presence was deemed contrary to public safety.

Quota Law of 1921

Limited the number of aliens of a particular nationality entering the United States to 3 percent of the foreign-born persons of that nationality who lived in the United States in 1910.

Act of 1922

Extended the Act of 1921 for two years, with amendments. Changed from one year to five years the residency requirement in a Western Hemisphere country. Authorized fines of transportation of inadmissible aliens.

Immigration Act of 1924

The first permanent limitation on immigration, established the "national origins quota system." In conjunction with the Immigration Act of 1917, governed American immigration policy until 1952.

Act of 1924

An appropriations law, provided for the establishment of the U.S. Border Patrol.

Act of March 1928

Provided more time to work out computation of the quotas established by the Immigration Act of 1924 by postponing introduction of the quotas until July 1, 1929.

Act of April 1928

Provided that the Immigration Act of 1924 was not to be construed to limit the right of American Indians to cross the border but with the proviso that the right does not extend to members of Indian tribes by adoption.

Registry Act of 1929

Amended existing immigration law authorizing the establishment of a record of lawful admission for certain aliens not ineligible for citizenship when no record of admission for permanent residence could be found and the alien could prove entrance before July 1, 1924.

Act of 1929

Added two deportable classes, aliens convicted of carrying any weapon or bomb and sentenced to any term of six months or more and aliens convicted of violation of the prohibition law for which a sentence of one year or more was imposed.

Act of 1931

Provided for the deportation of any alien convicted of violation of U.S. laws on the importation, exportation, manufacture, or sale of heroin, opium, or coca leaves.

Act of March 1932

Provided that the Contract Labor Laws were applicable to alien instrumental musicians entering the United States for permanent or temporary residence.

Act of May 1932

Amended the Immigration Act of 1917, doubling the allocation for enforcement for the Contract Labor Laws.

Act of July 1, 1932

Amended the Immigration Act of 1924, providing that the specified classes of nonimmigrant aliens be admitted for a prescribed period of time and under such conditions, including bonding where deemed necessary, as would ensure departure at the expiration of the prescribed time or on failure to maintain the status under which admitted.

Act of July 11, 1932

Provided exemption from quota limits to the husbands of American citizens, provided that the marriage occurred prior to issuance of the visa and prior to July 1, 1932. Wives of citizens were accorded nonquota status regardless of the time of marriage.

Act of June 15, 1935

Designated as a protection for American seamen. Repealed the laws giving privileges of citizenship regarding service on and protection by American vessels to aliens having their first papers.

Act of May 14, 1937

Made deportable any alien who at any time after entering the United States was found to have secured a visa through fraud by contracting a marriage which subsequent to entry into the United States had been judicially annulled retroactively to the date of the marriage; or failed or refused to fulfill his promises for a marital agreement made to procure his entry as an immigrant.

Act of June 14, 1940

Presidential Reorganization Plan. Transferred the Immigration and Naturalization Service from the Department of Labor to the Department of Justice as a national security measure.

Alien Registration Act of June 28, 1940

Required registration of all aliens and fingerprinting of those over fourteen years of age, established additional deportable classes, and authorized voluntary departure in lieu of deportation.

Act of July 1, 1940

Amended the Immigration Act of 1924, requiring aliens admitted as officials of foreign governments to maintain their status or depart.

Nationality Act of October 14, 1940

Codified and revised the naturalization, citizenship, and expatriation laws to strengthen the national defense. The naturalization and nationality regulations were rewritten and the forms used in naturalization proceedings were revised.

Public Safety Act of June 20, 1941

Directed consular officers to refuse a visa to any alien seeking to enter the United States for the purpose of engaging in activities which would endanger the United States.

Act of June 21, 1941

Extended the Act of May 22, 1918. Gave the president the power, during a time of national emergency or war, to prevent departure from or entry into the United States.

Act of December 8, 1942

Amended the Immigration Act of 1927, altering the reporting procedure in suspension of deportation cases to require the attorney general to report such suspensions to Congress on the first and fifteenth of each month that Congress is in session.

Act of April 29, 1943

Provided for the importation of temporary agricultural laborers to the United States from North, South, and Central America to aid agriculture during World War II. This program was later extended through 1947 and then served as the legal basis of the Mexican Bracero Program, which lasted through 1964.

Act of December 17, 1943

Amended the Alien Registration Act of 1940, adding to the classes eligible for naturalization Chinese persons or persons of Chinese descent. A quota of 105 persons per year was established.

Act of February 14, 1944

Provided for the importation of temporary workers from countries in the Western Hemisphere pursuant to agreements with such countries for employment in industries and services essential to the war effort. Agreements were subsequently made with British Honduras, Jamaica, Barbados, and the British West Indies.

War Brides Act of December 28, 1945

Waived visa requirements and provisions of immigration law excluding physical and mental defectives when they concerned members of the American armed forces who, during World War II, had married nationals of foreign countries.

G.I. Fiancees Act of June 29, 1946

Facilitated the admission to the United States of fiance(e)s of members of the American armed forces.

Act of July 2, 1946

Amended the Immigration Act of 1917, granting the privilege of admission to the United States as quota immigrants and eligibility for naturalization races indigenous to India and persons of Filipino descent.

Act of August 9, 1946

Gave nonquota status to Chinese wives of American citizens.

Act of June 28, 1947

Extended by six months the attorney general's authority to admit alien fiance(e)s of veterans as temporary visitors pending marriage.

Act of May 25, 1948

Amended the Act of October 16, 1918, providing for the expulsions and exclusion of anarchists and similar classes and gave the attorney general powers similar to those the secretary of state had through the refusal of immigration visas.

Displaced Persons Act of June 25, 1948

First expression of U.S. policy for admitting persons fleeing persecution. Permitted the admission of up to 205,000 displaced persons during the two-year period beginning July 1, 1948. Aimed at reducing the problem created by the presence in Germany, Austria, and Italy of more than one million displaced persons.

Act of July 1, 1948

Made available suspension of deportation to aliens even though they were ineligible for naturalization by reason of race. Suspension of deportation included good moral character, approval of the attorney general, or residence in the United States for seven years or more.

Central Intelligence Agency Act of June 20, 1949

Authorized the admission of a limited number of aliens in the interest of national security.

Agricultural Act of October 31, 1949

Facilitated the entry of seasonal farm workers to meet labor shortages in the United States. Extension of the Mexican Bracero Program.

Act of June 16, 1950

Amended the Displaced Persons Act of 1948. Extended the act to June 30, 1951, and its application to war orphans and German expellees and refugees to July 1, 1952. Increased the total persons who could be admitted under the act to 415,744.

Act of June 30, 1950

Provided relief to the sheepherding industry by authorizing that, during a one-year period, 250 special quota immigration visas be issued to skilled sheepherders chargeable to oversubscribed quotas.

Act of August 19, 1950

Made spouses and minor children of members of the American armed forces, regardless of the alien's race, eligible for immigration and nonquota status if marriage occurred before March 19, 1952.

Internal Security Act of September 22, 1950

Amended various immigration laws with a view toward strengthening security screening in cases of aliens in the United States or applying for entry.

Act of March 28, 1951

Gave the attorney general authority to amend the record of certain aliens who were admitted only temporarily because of affiliations other than Communist.

Act of July 12, 1951

Amended the Agricultural Act of 1949, serving as the basic framework under which the Mexican Bracero Program operated until 1962. Provided that the U.S. government establish and operate reception centers at or near the Mexican border; provide transportation, subsistence, and medical care from the Mexican recruiting centers to the U.S. reception centers; and guarantee performance by employers in matters relating to transportation and wages, including all forms of remuneration. U.S. employers are to pay the prevailing wages in the area; guarantee the workers employment for three-fourths of the contract period; and provide workers with free housing and adequate meals at a reasonable cost.

Act of March 20, 1952

Amended the Immigration Act of 1917, making it a felony to bring in or willfully induce an alien unlawfully to enter or reside in the United States. However, the usual and normal practices incident to employment were not deemed to constitute harboring. Defined further the powers of the Border Patrol, giving officers of the Immigration and Naturalization Service authority to have access to private lands, but not dwellings, within twenty-five miles of an external boundary for the purpose of patrolling the border to prevent the illegal entry of aliens.

Act of April 9, 1952

Added the issuance of five hundred immigration visas to sheepherders.

Immigration and Naturalization Act of June 27, 1952

Brought into one comprehensive statute the multiple laws which, before its enactment, governed immigration and naturalization in the United States. In general, perpetuated the immigration policies from earlier statutes with modifications; for example, it made all races eligible for naturalization, thus eliminating race as a bar to immigration. Eliminated discrimination between sexes with respect to immigration.

Refugee Relief Act of August 7, 1953

Authorized the issuance of special nonquota visas allowing 214,000 aliens to become permanent residents of the United States, in addition to those whose admission was authorized by the Immigration and Nationality Act of 1952.

Act of September 3, 1954

Made special nonquota immigrant visas available to certain skilled sheepherders for a period of up to one year. Exempted from inadmissibility to the United States aliens who had committed no more than one petty offense.

Act of September 3, 1954

Provided for the expatriation of persons convicted of engaging in a conspiracy to overthrow or levy war against the U.S. government.

Act of July 24, 1957

Permitted enlistment of aliens into the regular army.

Act of August 30, 1957

Exempted aliens who were survivors of certain deceased members of the U.S. Armed Forces from provisions of the Social Security Act which prohibited the payment of benefits to aliens outside the United States.

Refugee-Escapee Act of September 11, 1957

Addressed the problem of quota oversubscription by removing the "mortgaging" of immigrant quotas imposed under the Displaced Persons Act of 1948 and other subsequent acts.

Act of July 25, 1958

Granted admission for permanent residence to Hungarian parolees of at least two years' residence in the United States, on condition that the alien was admissible at time of entry and still admissible.

Act of August 21, 1958

Authorized the attorney general to adjust nonimmigrant aliens from temporary to permanent resident status subject to visa availability.

Act of September 22, 1958

Facilitated the entry of fiance(e)s and relatives of alien residents and citizens of the United States by reclassifying certain categories of relatives into preference portions of the immigration quotas. This was designed to assist in reuniting families both on a permanent basis, through the amendments to the Immigration and Nationality Act of 1952, and through temporary programs.

Act of July 14, 1960

"Fair Share Refugee Act." Authorized the attorney general to parole up to five hundred alien refugee-escapees and make them eligible for permanent residence.

Act of August 17, 1961

Provided that, in peacetime, no volunteer is to be accepted into the army or air force unless the person is a citizen or an alien admitted for permanent residence.

Act of September 26, 1961

Liberalized the quota provisions of the Immigration and Nationality Act of 1952. Eliminated the ceiling of two thousand on the aggregate quota of the Asia-Pacific triangle.

Act of October 24, 1962

Granted nonquota immigrant visas for certain aliens eligible for fourth preference (i.e., brothers, sisters, and children of citizens) and for first preference (i.e., aliens with special occupational skills).

Act of December 13, 1963

Extended the Mexican Bracero Program one additional year to December 31, 1964.

Immigration and Nationality Act Amendments of October 3, 1965

Abolished the national origins quota system, eliminating national origin, race, or ancestry as a basis for immigration to the United States.

Freedom of Information Act of July 4, 1966

Established that the record of every proceeding before the INS in an individual's case be made available to the alien or his attorney of record.

Act of November 2, 1966

Authorized the attorney general to adjust the status of Cuban refugees to that of permanent resident alien, chargeable to the 120,000 annual limit for the Western Hemisphere.

Act of November 6, 1966

Extended the derivative citizenship to children born on or after December 24, 1952, of civilian U.S. citizens serving abroad. Provided that time spent abroad by U.S. citizens in the employ of the U.S. government or certain international organizations could be treated as physical presence in the United States for the purpose of transmitting U.S. citizenship to children born abroad.

Act of December 18, 1967

Facilitated the expeditious naturalization of certain noncitizen employees of U.S. nonprofit organizations.

Act of June 19, 1968

Omnibus crime control and safe streets legislation. Declared it illegal for aliens who are illegally in the country and for former citizens who have renounced their citizenship to receive, possess, or transport a firearm.

Act of October 24, 1968

Amended the Immigration and Nationality Act of 1952, providing for expeditious naturalization of noncitizens who have rendered service in the U.S. armed forces during the Vietnam conflict or in other periods of military hostilities.

Act of April 7, 1970

Created two new classes of nonimmigrant admission, fiance(e)s of U.S. citizens and intracompany transferees.

Act of August 10, 1971

Amended the Communications Act of 1934, providing that lawful permanent resident aliens be permitted to operate amateur radio stations in the United States and hold licenses for their stations.

Act of September 28, 1971

Amended the Selective Service Act of 1967. Registration for the selective service shall be applicable to any alien admitted to the United States as a nonimmigrant as long as he continues to maintain a lawful nonimmigrant status in the United States.

Act of October 27, 1972

Reduced restrictions concerning residence requirements for retention of U.S. citizenship acquired by birth abroad through a U.S. citizen parent and an alien parent.

Social Security Act Amendments of October 30, 1972

Amended the Social Security Act, providing that Social Security numbers be assigned to aliens at the time of their lawful admission to the United States for permanent residence or temporarily to engage in lawful employment.

Act of October 20, 1974

Repealed the "Coolie Trade" legislation of 1862. Such legislation, passed to protect Chinese and Japanese aliens from exploitation caused by discriminatory treatment from immigration laws then in effect, had become virtually inoperative because most of the laws singling out Oriental peoples had been repealed or modified.

Indochina Migration and Refugee Assistance Act of May 23, 1975

Established a program of domestic resettlement assistance for refugees who had fled from Cambodia and Vietnam.

Act of July 21, 1976

Made Laotians eligible for programs established by the Indochina Migration and Refugee Assistance Act of 1975.

Act of October 12, 1976

Placed restrictions on foreign medical school graduates (both immigrants and nonimmigrants) coming to the United States for practice or training in the medical professions. Effective January 10, 1977.

Immigration and Nationality Act Amendments of October 20, 1976

Applied the same twenty-thousand-person-per-country limit to the Western Hemisphere as applied to the Eastern Hemisphere.

Act of October 20, 1976

Denied unemployment compensation to aliens not lawfully admitted for permanent residence or otherwise permanently residing in the United States under color of law.

Act of August 1, 1977

Eased restrictions on foreign medical school graduates; for example, it exempted aliens who are of national or international renown in the field of medicine and certain alien physicians already in the United States from the examination requirement.

Act of October 28, 1977

Permitted adjustment to permanent resident status for Indochinese refugees who are natives or citizens of Vietnam, Laos, or Cambodia, were physically present in the United States for at least two years, and were admitted or paroled into the United States during specified periods of time. Extended the time limit during which refugee assistance may be provided to such refugees.

Act of October 5, 1978

Combined the separate ceilings for Eastern and Western Hemisphere immigration into one worldwide limit of 290,000.

Act of October 5, 1978

Made several changes pertaining to the adoption of alien children, including permission for U.S. citizens to petition for the classification of more than two alien orphans as immediate relatives.

Act of October 7, 1978

Made permanent the president's authority to regulate the entry of aliens and to require U.S. citizens to bear valid passports when entering or leaving the United States.

Act of October 14, 1978

Required any alien who acquires or transfers any interest in agricultural land to submit a report to the secretary of agriculture within ninety days after acquisition or transfer.

Act of October 30, 1978

Provided for the exclusion and expulsion of aliens who persecuted others on the basis of race, religion, national origin, or political opinion under the direction of the Nazi government of Germany or its allies.

Act of November 2, 1978

Provided for the seizure and forfeiture of vessels, vehicles, and aircraft used in smuggling aliens or knowingly transporting aliens to the United States illegally. An exception was made where the owner or person in control did not consent to the illegal act.

Panama Canal Act of September 27, 1979

Allowed admission as permanent residents to certain aliens with employment on or before 1977 with the Panama Canal Company, the Canal Zone government, or the U.S. government in the Canal Zone and their families.

Refugee Act of March 17, 1980

Provided the first permanent and systematic procedure for the admission and effective resettlement of refugees of special humanitarian concern to the United States.

Refugee Education Assistance Act of October 10, 1980

Established a program of formula grants to state education agencies for basic education of refugee children. Also provided for services to Cuban and Haitian entrants identical to those for refugees under the Refugee Act of 1980.

Act of June 5, 1981

Supplemental appropriations and recessions bill which reduced previously appropriated funds for migration and refugee assistance, including funds provided for reception and processing of Cuban and Haitian entrants.

Act of August 13, 1981

Federal appropriations bill for fiscal year 1982, also contained items restricting the access of aliens to various publicly funded benefits. Severely restricted eligibility to aliens for Aid to Families with Dependent Children.

Immigration and Nationality Act Amendments of December 20, 1981

"INS Efficiency Bill." Amended the Immigration and Nationality Act of 1952 and the Act of November 2, 1978. Authorized the INS to seize vehicles without having to establish whether the owner was involved in the illegal activity in question.

Act of September 30, 1982

Allowed admission as permanent residents to certain nonimmigrant aliens residing in the Virgin Islands.

Act of October 2, 1982

Greatly limited the categories of aliens to whom the Legal Services Corporation may provide legal assistance.

Act of October 22, 1982

Provided that children born of U.S. citizen fathers in Korea, Vietnam, Laos, Kampuchea, or Thailand after 1950 and before enactment may come to the United States as immediate relatives or as first or fourth preference immigrants.

Immigration Reform and Control Act of November 6, 1986 (IRCA)

Authorized the legalization (i.e., temporary and then permanent resident status) for aliens who had resided in the United States in an unlawful status since January 1, 1982; created sanctions prohibiting employers from knowingly hiring, recruiting, or referring for a fee aliens not authorized to work in the United States; and increased enforcement at U.S. borders.

Immigration Marriage Fraud Amendments of November 10, 1986

Stipulated that aliens deriving their immigrant status based on a marriage of less than two years are conditional immigrants.

AmerAsian Homecoming Act of December 22, 1987

An appropriations law prohibiting admission of children born in Vietnam between specified dates to Vietnamese mothers and American fathers, together with their immediate relatives. They are admitted as nonquota immigrants but receive refugee program benefits.

Act of September 28, 1988

United States–Canada Free Trade Agreement Implementation Act. Facilitated temporary entry on a reciprocal basis between the United States and Canada. Established procedures for the temporary entry into the United States of Canadian citizen professional businesspersons to render services for remuneration.

Act of November 15, 1988

Provided for the extension of stay for certain nonimmigrant H-1 nurses.

Foreign Operations Act of November 21, 1989

An appropriations law which provided for adjustment to permanent resident status for Soviet and Indochinese nationals who were paroled into the United States between certain dates after denial of refugee status.

Act of December 18, 1989

Immigration Nursing Relief Act of 1989. Adjustment from temporary to permanent resident status, without regard to numerical limitation, of certain nonimmigrants who were employed in the United States as registered nurses for at least three years and meet established certification standards.

Immigration Act of November 29, 1990

Revised all grounds for exclusion and deportation, significantly rewriting the political and ideological grounds. Authorized the attorney general to grant temporary protected status to undocumented alien nationals of designated countries subject to armed conflict or natural disasters.

Armed Forces Immigration Adjustment Act of October 1, 1991

Granted special immigrant status to certain types of aliens who honorably served in the armed forces of the United States for at least twelve years.

Act of December 12, 1991

Miscellaneous and Technical Immigration and Naturalization Amendments Act. Amended certain elements of the Immigration Act of 1990.

Chinese Student Protection Act of October 9, 1992

Provided for adjustment to permanent resident status (as employment-based immigrants) by nationals of the People's Republic of China who were in the United States after June 4, 1989, and before April 11, 1990.

Soviet Scientists Immigration Act of October 10, 1992

Conferred permanent resident status (as employment-based immigrants) on a maximum of seven hundred fifty scientists from the independent states of the former Soviet Union and the Baltic states. The limit does not include spouses and children.

North American Free Trade Agreement Implementation Act of December 8, 1993

Supersedes the United States–Canada Free Trade Agreement Act of September 28, 1988. Facilitated temporary entry on a reciprocal basis between the United States and Canada and Mexico. Established the procedures for the temporary entry into the United States of Canadian and Mexican citizen professional businesspersons to render services for remuneration.

Violent Crimes Control and Law Enforcement Act of September 13, 1994

Authorized the establishment of a criminal alien tracking center. Established a new nonimmigrant classification for alien witness cooperation and counterterrorism information.

Anti-Terrorism and Effective Death Penalty Act of April 24, 1996

Expedited procedures for the removal of alien terrorists. Established specific measures to exclude members and representatives of terrorist organizations.

Personal Responsibility and Work Opportunity Reconciliation Act of August 22, 1996

Established restrictions on the eligibility of legal immigrants for means-tested public assistance. Broadened the restrictions on public benefits for illegal aliens and nonimmigrants.

Illegal Immigration Reform and Immigrant Responsibility Act of September 30, 1996

Established measures to control U.S. borders, protect legal workers through worksite enforcement, and remove criminal and other deportable aliens. Placed added restrictions on benefits for aliens.

Notes

Chapter One

1. In this work, I use the term "undocumented immigrant" to refer to immigrants who are in the country illegally. The term "illegal alien" is used by the Immigration and Naturalization Service.

2. To investigate our hypotheses, we conducted a content analysis of political candidates' statements as quoted in mainstream newspapers between January 1, 1993, and December 31, 1999. The source of our data is Lexis-Nexus, an electronic database containing full-text newspaper articles from around the world. For purposes of this study, the search was restricted to references to what U.S. politicians said concerning Mexican immigration. These statements were either direct quotations or journalistic summaries. No opinion editorials were used.

The initial search on the database used the key terms "candidate" and "immigrant." This produced several thousand articles, many of which were not relevant to the study. For example, the search may have produced an article on a "candidate" who may have been the son or daughter of an "immigrant." To limit the search, the term "Mexican" was added to "immigrant," and "candidate." The final combination used to gather our data was "Candidate" as the keyword and "Immigrant and Mexican" as the additional search terms. This produced a sample of 917 articles. We then eliminated any double articles or articles that did not fit the study. For instance, our search produced some articles that had a "candidate" in England discussing "Mexican immigration" in the United States. In addition, we eliminated any syndicated articles that may have appeared in more than one newspaper. This produced a final sample of 415 articles. It should be noted that using an electronic database such as that generated by Lexis-Nexus has inherent limitations. To ensure reliability for our search terms, we ran ten trials using the same terms in order. The exact number of articles surfaced for each trial. Therefore, we are confident that the database is reliable as long as the order of the input terms is consistent.

Previous research on this topic guided the categories generated with which to content analyze the population of articles (Short and Magaña 2002). There were predominantly four categories of issues that characterized immigration issues as a political platform during the years 1993 to 1999: economic, legal, cultural, and electoral. Furthermore, it was necessary to specify if the theme talked about or reported on in the newspaper had a "negative" or "positive" valence associated with it. For instance, economic issues with respect to Mexican immigration could possess a negative valence, highlighting such issues as stealing social services and American jobs and costing taxpayers, or a positive valence such as Mexican immigrants' contribution to the tax base, successful entrepreneurship, and the like. Also some articles contained both a positive and a negative valence. With these themes in mind, we approached all the articles using the codebook in Appendix B. We chose not to limit our analysis to any one unit—that is, words, sentences, phrases, and so on—as we felt this could jeopardize the context in which candidate statements were reported.

Chapter Two

1. Most of the following history has been taken from the INS report "Whom We Shall Welcome," by the President's Commission on Immigration and Naturalization.

2. The United States Constitution does not discuss deterring undocumented immigration.

3. The term "Wetback" refers to Mexican undocumented immigrants who migrate via the Rio Grande.

4. Scholars have maintained that these numbers were highly inflated by the INS so as to give the impression that they had successfully completed the operation.

Chapter Three

1. On many occasions I have heard Mexican nationals refer to Hispanic INS agents as the worst or most insensitive to their needs.

Glossary

Alien Any person not a citizen or national of the United States.

Apprehension The arrest of a deportable alien by the Immigration and Naturalization Service. Each apprehension of the same alien in a fiscal year is counted separately.

Asylee An alien in the United States or at a port of entry unable or unwilling to return to his or her country of nationality, or to seek the protection of that country because of persecution or a well-founded fear of persecution. Persecution or the fear thereof may be based on the alien's race, religion, nationality, membership in a particular social group, or political opinion. For persons with no nationality, the country of nationality is considered to be the country in which the alien last habitually resided. Asylees are eligible to adjust to lawful permanent resident status after one year of continuous presence in the United States. The immigrants are limited to ten thousand adjustments per fiscal year.

Beneficiarie Those aliens who receive immigration benefits from petitions filed with the U.S. Immigration and Naturalization Service. Beneficiaries generally derive privilege or status as a result of their relationship (including that of employer-employee) to a U.S. citizen or lawful permanent resident.

Border Patrol Sector Any one of twenty-one geographic areas into which the United States is divided for the Immigration and Naturalization Service's Border Patrol activities.

Deportable Alien An alien in the United States subject to any of the five grounds of deportation specified in the Immigration and Nationality Act. This includes any alien illegally in the United States, regardless of whether the alien entered the country illegally or entered legally but subsequently violated the terms of his or her visa.

Deportation The formal removal of an alien from the United States when the presence of that alien is deemed inconsistent with the public welfare. Deportation is ordered by an immigration judge without any punishment being imposed or contemplated.

District Any one of the thirty-three geographic areas into which the United States and its territories are divided for the Immigration and Naturalization Service's field operations or one of three overseas offices located in Rome, Bangkok, or Mexico City. Operations are supervised by a district director located at a district office within the district's geographic boundaries.

Employer Sanctions   The employer sanctions provision of the Immigration Reform and Control Act of 1986 prohibits employers from hiring, recruiting, or referring for a fee aliens known to be unauthorized to work in the United States. Violators of the law are subject to a series of civil fines or criminal penalties when there is a pattern of practice of violations.

Immigrant   An alien admitted to the United States as a lawful permanent resident. Immigrants are those persons lawfully accorded the privilege of residing permanently in the United States. They may be issued immigrant visas by the Department of State overseas or adjusted to permanent resident status by the Immigration and Naturalization Service in the United States.

Immigration Reform and Control Act (IRCA) of 1986—Public Law 99-603 (Act of November 6, 1986), which was passed in order to control and deter illegal immigration to the United States. Its major provisions stipulate legalization of undocumented aliens, legalization of certain agricultural workers, sanctions for employers who knowingly hire undocumented workers, and increased enforcement at U.S. borders.

Legalized Aliens   Certain illegal aliens who were eligible to apply for temporary resident status under the legalization provision of the Immigration Reform and Control Act of 1986. To be eligible, aliens must have continuously resided in the United States in an unlawful status since January 1, 1982, not be excludable, and have entered the United States either (1) illegally before January 1, 1982, or (2) as temporary visitors before January 1, 1982, with their authorized stay expiring before that date or with the government's knowledge of their unlawful status before that date. Legalization consists of two stages—temporary and then permanent residency. To adjust to permanent status aliens must have had continuous residence in the United States, be admissible as an immigrant, and demonstrate at least a minimal understanding and knowledge of the English language and U.S. history and government.

Nonimmigrant   An alien who seeks temporary entry to the United States for a specific purpose. The alien must have a permanent residence abroad (for most classes of admission) and qualify for the nonimmigrant classification sought. The nonimmigrant classifications are foreign government officials, visitors for business and for pleasure, aliens in transit through the United States, treaty traders, and investors, students, international representatives, temporary workers and trainees, representatives of foreign information media, exchange visitors, finance(e)s of U.S. citizens, intracompany transferees, and NATO officials. Most nonimmigrants can be accompanied or joined by spouses and unmarried minor (or dependent) children. Although refugees, parolees, withdrawals, and stowaways are processed as nonimmigrants on arrival to the United States, these classes, as well as crewmen, are not included in nonimmigrant admission data.

Naturalization   The conferring, by any means, of citizenship upon a person after birth.

Naturalization Provisions   The basic requirements for naturalization that every applicant must meet, unless a member of a special class. General provisions require an applicant to be at least eighteen years of age, a lawful permanent resident with five years of continuous residence in the United States, and to have been physically present in the country for half that period.

Port of Entry   Any location in the United States or its territories which is designated as a point of entry for aliens and U.S. citizens. All district and field control offices are also considered ports since they become locations of entry for aliens adjusting to immigrant status.

Preference System (prior to fiscal year 1992)—The six categories among which 270,000 immigrant visa numbers are distributed each year during the period 1981–1991. This preference system was amended by the Immigration Act of 1990, effective fiscal year 1992. (See Preference System (Immigration Act of 1990.) The six categories were unmarried sons and daughters (over twenty-one years of age) of U.S. citizens (20 percent); spouses and unmarried sons and daughters of aliens lawfully admitted for permanent residence (26 percent); members of the professions or persons of exceptional ability in the sciences and the arts (10 percent); brothers and sisters of U.S. citizens over twenty-one years of age (24 percent); and needed skilled or unskilled workers (10 percent). A nonpreference category, historically open to immigrants not entitled to a visa number under one of the six preferences just listed, had no numbers available beginning in September 1978.

Preference System (Immigration Act of 1990)   The nine categories since fiscal year 1992 among which the family-sponsored and employment-based immigrant preference visas are distributed. The family-sponsored preferences are (1)unmarried sons and daughters of U.S. citizens; (2) spouses, children, and unmarried sons and daughters of permanent resident aliens; and (3) married sons and daughters of U.S. citizens. The employment based preferences are (1) priority workers (persons of extraordinary ability, outstanding professors and researchers, and certain multinational executives and managers); (2) professionals with advanced degrees or aliens with exceptional ability; and (3) skilled workers and professionals (without advanced degrees). The number of visas issued annually may vary.

Refugee   Any person who is outside his or her country of nationality who is unable or unwilling to return to that country because of persecution or a well-founded fear of persecution. Persecution or the fear thereof may be based on the alien's race, religion, nationality, membership in a particular social group, or political opinion. People with no nationality must be outside their country of last habitual residence to qualify as a refugee. Refugees are exempt from numerical limitation (though worldwide ceilings by geographic area are set annually by the president) and are eligible to adjust to lawful permanent residence after one year of continuous presence in the United States.

Although these aliens are considered nonimmigrants when initially admitted to the United States, refugees are not included in nonimmigrant admission.

Region   Any one of three areas of the United States—Eastern Region, Central Region, and Western Region—into which the Immigration and Naturalization Service divides jurisdiction for operational purposes.

Registry   Aliens who have continuously resided in the United States in unlawful status since January 1, 1972, are eligible to adjust to legal permanent resident status under the registry provision. Before the Immigration Reform and Control Act of 1986, aliens had to have been in the country continuously since June 30, 1948, to qualify.

Special Agricultural Workers (SAW)—Aliens who performed labor in perishable agricultural commodities for a specified period of time and were admitted for temporary and then permanent residence under a provision of the Immigration Reform and Control Act of 1986. Up to 350,000 aliens who worked at least ninety days in each of the three years preceding May 1, 1986, were eligible for Group II temporary resident status. Adjustment to permanent resident status is essentially automatic for both groups; however, aliens in Group I were eligible on December 1, 1989, and those in Group II were eligible one year later, on December 1, 1990.

Temporary Protective Status (TPS)—Establishes a legislative base to the administrative practice of allowing a group of persons temporary refuge in the United States. Under a provision of the Immigration Act of 1990, the attorney general may designate nationals of a foreign state to be eligible for TPS with a finding that conditions in that country pose a danger to personal safety due to ongoing armed conflict or an environmental disaster. The legislation designated El Salvador as the first country to qualify for this program. Deportation proceedings are suspended against aliens while they are in Temporary Protective status.

Temporary Worker   An alien worker coming to the United States to work for a temporary period of time. The Immigration Reform and Control Act of 1986, the Immigration Nursing Relief Act of 1989, and the Immigration Act of 1990 revised existing classes and created new classes of nonimmigrant admission. Nonimmigrant worker classes of admission are as follows:

H-1A   registered nurses

H-1B   workers with "specialty occupation" admitted on the basis of professional education, skills, and/or equivalent experience

H-2B   temporary agricultural workers coming to the United States to perform agricultural services or labor of a temporary or seasonal nature when services are unavailable in the United States

H-2B   temporary nonagricultural workers coming to the United States to perform temporary services or labor if unemployed persons capable of performing the service or labor cannot be found in the United States

H-3   aliens coming temporarily to the United States as trainees other than to receive graduate medical education or training

O-1, O-2, O-3   temporary workers with extraordinary ability in the sciences, arts, education, business, or athletics; those entering solely for the purpose of accompanying and assisting such workers; and their spouses and children

P-1, P-2, P-3, P-4   athletes and entertainers at an internationally recognized level of performance; artists and entertainers under a reciprocal exchange program; artists and entertainers under a program that is "culturally unique," and their spouses and children

Q   participants in international cultural exchange programs

R-1, R-2   temporary workers to perform work in religious occupations and their spouses and children. Temporary visitors in the Exchange Visitor, Intracompany Transferee, and U.S.-Canada or North American Free Trade Agreement classes of nonimmigrant admission also are granted authorization to work temporarily in the United States.

Undocumented Immigrant   Any person not a citizen or national of the United States who entered the country illegally.

References

Andraes, P. 1998. The U.S. immigration control offensive: Constructing an image of order on the Southwest border. In *Crossings: Mexican Immigration in Interdisciplinary Perspectives*, ed. M. M. Suarez-Orozco. Cambridge, Mass.: Harvard University Press.

Apodaga, C., and M. Stohl. 1999. United States human rights policy and foreign assistance. *International Studies Quarterly* 43: 185–198.

Baker-Gonzalez, S. 1990. *The Cautious Welcome: The Legalization Programs of the Immigration Reform and Control Act*. Santa Monica, Calif.: RAND Corporation.

Ball, H. 1984. *Administrative Agencies: Essays on Power and Politics*. Englewood, N.J.: Prentice Hall.

Bardach, E. 1977. *Implementation Game*. Cambridge, Mass.: MIT Press.

Bardarch, E., and R. A. Kagan. 1982. *Going by the Book*. Philadelphia: Temple University Press.

Bean, F. 1990. *Undocumented Migration to the United States: IRCA and the Experience of the 1980's*. Washington, D.C.: Urban Institute.

Bodnar, J. E. 1987. *The Transplanted: A History of Immigrants in Urban America*. Bloomington: Indiana University Press.

Briggs, V. M., Jr. 1984. *Immigration Policy and the American Labor Force*. Baltimore: Johns Hopkins University Press.

———. 1992. *Mass Immigration and the National Interest*. New York: M. E. Sharpe.

Briggs, V. M., and S. Moore. 1994. *Still an Open Door? U.S. Immigration Policy and the American Economy*. Washington, D.C.: American University Press.

Bullock, C., and C. Lamb. 1984. *Implementation of Civil Rights Policy*. Belmont, Calif.: Wadsworth.

Calavita, K. 1992. *Inside the State: The Bracero Program, Immigration, and the INS*. New York: Routledge.

Chin, K. L. 1999. *Smuggled Chinese: Clandestine Immigration to the United States*. Philadelphia: Temple University Press.

Comprehensive Adult Student Assessment System. 1989. *A Survey of Newly Legalized Persons in California*. Prepared for the California Health and Welfare Agency.

Congressional Hispanic Caucus Report. 1994. "Fact and Fiction: Immigrants in the U.S." October 7.

Cornelius, W. A. 1989. The U.S. demand for Mexican labor. In *Mexican Migration to the United States: Origins, Consequences, and Policy Options*, ed. W. A. Cornelius and J. A. Bustamante, 25–47. La Jolla: University of California, San Diego, Center for U.S.-Mexican Studies.

———. 1998. The structural embeddedness of demand for Mexican immigrant labor: New evidence from California. In *Crossings: Mexican Immigration in Interdisciplinary Perspectives*, ed. M. M. Suarez-Orozco, 113–115. Cambridge, Mass.: Harvard University Press.

Crane, K., B. Asch, J. Helbrunn, and D. Cullinane. 1990. *The Effect of Employer Sanctions on the Flow of Undocumented Immigrants to the United States.* Santa Monica, Calif.: RAND Corporation.

Curtis, C. M. 1997. Factors influencing parents' perceptions of child care services: Implications for public policy formulation. *Journal of Black Studies* 27: 6.

Daniel, C. E. 1981. *Bitter Harvest: A History of California Farmworkers, 1870–1941.* Ithaca: Cornell University Press.

de la Torre, A., and A. L. Estrada. 2001. *Mexican Americans and Health: Sana! Sana!* Tucson: University of Arizona Press.

Derthick, M. 1990. *Agency under Stress: The Social Security Administration in American Government.* Washington, D.C.: Brookings Institution.

De Sipio, L., and R. O. de la Garza. 1998. *Making Americans and Remaking America.* Boulder, Colo.: Westview Press.

Dovidio, J. F., and S. L. Gaertner. 1983. The effects of sex, status, and ability on helping behavior. *Journal of Applied Social Psychology* 13: 191–205.

———. 1986. Prejudice, discrimination, and racism: Historical trends and contemporary approaches. In *Prejudice, Discrimination, and Racism*, ed. J. F. Dovidio and S. L. Gaertner, 1–34. Orlando, Fla.: Academic Press.

———. 1996. Affirmative action, unintentional racial biases, and intergroup relations. *Journal of Social Issues* 52(4): 51–76.

Dovidio, J. F., S. L. Gaertner, P. A. Anastasio, and R. Sanitioso. 1992. Cognitive and motivational bases of bias: The implications of aversive racism for attitudes toward Hispanics. In *Hispanics in the Workplace*, ed. S. Knouse, P. Rosenfeld, and A. Culbertson, 75–106. Newbury Park, Calif.: Sage.

Dunn, T. J. 1996. *The Militarization of the U.S.-Mexico Border, 1978–1992.* Austin: Center for Mexican American Studies.

Espenshade, J., and M. Belanger. 1998. Immigration and public opinion. In *Crossings: Mexican Immigration in Interdisciplinary Perspectives*, ed. M. M. Suarez-Orozco, 363–382. Cambridge, Mass.: Harvard University Press.

Fix, M. E., and J. S. Passel. 1994. *Immigration and Immigrants: Setting the Record Straight.* Washington, D.C.: Urban Institute.

Gaertner, S. L. and J. F. Dovidio. 1977. The subtlety of white racism, arousal, and helping behavior. *Journal of Personality and Social Psychology* 35: 691–707.

———. 1986. The aversive form of racism. In *Prejudice, Discrimination, and Racism: Theory and Research*, ed. J. F. Dovidio and S. L. Gaertner, 61–89. Orlando, Fla.: Academic Press.

Garcia, Juan Ramon G. 1980. *Operation Wetback*. Westport, Conn.: Greenwood Press.

General Accounting Office (GAO). 1988. *Immigration Reform: Status of Implementing Employer Sanctions after Second Years*. Report to Congress. November. Washington, D.C.

———. 1990. *Immigration Reform: Employer Sanctions and the Question of Discrimination*. Report to Congress. March. Washington, D.C.

———. 1991. *Immigration Management: Strong Leadership and Management Reforms Needed to Address Serious Problems*. Report to Congress. January. Washington D.C.

Goggin, M., A. O'M. Bowman, J. Lester, and L. O'Toole. 1990. *Implementation Theory and Practice: Toward a Third Generation*. Boston: Scott Foresman/ Little, Brown.

Gutierrez, D. G. 1995. *Walls and Mirrors: Mexican Americans, Mexican Immigrants, and the Politics of Ethnicity*. Berkeley: University of California Press.

Hagan, J. M., and S. Baker-Gonzales. 1991. Implementing the U.S. legalization program: The influence of immigrant communities and local agencies on immigration reform. *International Migration Review* 27(3): 513–536.

Hamamoto, D. Y., and R. D. Torres. 1997. *New American Destinies: A Reader in Contemporary Asian and Latino Immigration*. New York: Routledge.

Handlin, O. 1954. *The American People in the Twentieth Century*. Cambridge, Mass.: Harvard University Press.

Hargrove, E., and J. Glidwell. 1990. *Impossible Jobs in Public Management*. Lawrence: University Press of Kansas.

Heritage Foundation. 1989. *The Immigration Impact*. Washington, D.C.: Heritage Foundation.

Higham, J. 1988. *Strangers in the Land: Patterns of American Nativism, 1860–1925*. New Brunswick, N.J.: Rutgers University Press.

Hondaneu-Sotelo, P. 1994. *Gendered Transitions*. Berkeley: University of California Press.

Hutchinson, E. P. 1981. *Legislative History of American Immigration Policy, 1798–1966*. Philadelphia: University of Pennsylvania Press.

Immigration Statistics: Information Gaps, Quality Issues Limit Utility of Federal Data to Policymakers (Chapter Report, 07/31/98, GAO/GGD-98-164).

INS Web site. http://www.ins.usdoj.gov/graphics/index.htm.

Juffras, J. 1991. *Impact of the Immigration Reform and Control Act on the Immigration and Naturalization Service*. Santa Monica, Calif.: RAND Corporation.

Kahn, R. S. 1996. *Other People's Blood*. Boulder, Colo.: Westview Press.

Kanter, R. 1983. *The Change Masters*. New York: Simon and Schuster.

Lindenberg, K. E. 2000. Sexual harassment: Successful policy implementation. *IQ-Service Report* 32: 1–12.

Lipsky, M. 1971. Toward street-level bureaucracy. *Urban Affairs* 4: 196–213.

———. 1980. *Street-level Bureaucracy: Dilemmas of the Individual in Public Services*. New York: Russell Sage Foundation.

Manheim, J. B., and R. C. Rich. 1981. *Empirical Political Analysis: Research Methods in Political Science*. Englewood Cliffs, N.J: Prentice-Hall.

Massey, D. S., R. Alarcon, H. Gonzalez, and J. Durand. 1987. *Return to Aztlan: The Social Process of International Migration from Western Mexico*. Berkeley: University California Press.

Mazmanian, D., and P. A. Sabatier. 1989. *Implementation of Public Policy*. Lanham, Md.: University Press of America.

McConahay, J. B. 1986. Modern racism, ambivalence, and the modern racism scale. In *Prejudice, Discrimination, and Racism*, ed. J. F. Dovidio and S. L. Gaertner, 91–125. Orlando, Fla.: Academic Press.

Menjivar, C. 2000. *Fragmented Ties: Salvadoran Immigrant Networks in America*. Berkeley: University of California Press.

Middleton, M. 1997. Information policy and infrastructure in Australia. *Journal of Government Information* 24: 9–25.

Montwieler, N. 1986. *The Immigration Reform Law of 1986: Analysis, Text, and Legislative History*. Washington, D.C: Bureau of National Affairs.

Moore, J., and H. Pachon. 1985. *Hispanics in the United States*. Englewood Cliffs, N.J.: Prentice-Hall.

Morales, R., and F. Bonilla. 1993. *Latinos in a Changing U.S. Economy*. Thousand Oaks, Calif.: Sage.

Morris, M. 1985. *The Beleaguered Bureaucracy*. Washington, D.C: Brookings Institution.

Muñoz, C. 1990. *Unfinished Business: The Immigration Reform and Control Act of 1986*. Washington, D.C.: National Council of La Raza.

Nakamura, R. T., and F. Smallwood. 1980. *The Politics of Policy Implementation*. New York: St. Martin's Press.

National Academy of Administration. 1991. Managerial options for the immigration and naturalization service. A Report to the United States Department of Justice. February.

National Association of Latino Elected Officials (NALEO). 1989. *The National Latino Immigrant Survey*. Washington, D.C.: NALEO.

National Center for Immigrants' Rights. 1988. Special Legalization Wrap-up Issue. *Immigration Law Bulletin*. Los Angeles.

National Research Council. 1997. *The New Americans: Economic, Demographic, and Fiscal Effects of Immigration*. Washington, D.C.: National Academy Press.

North, D. S., and M. Portz. 1989. *Decision Factories: The Role of the Regional Processing Facilities in the Alien Legalization Programs*. Report prepared for the consideration of the Administrative Conference of the United States.

Ong Hing, B. 1993. *Making and Remaking Asian America through Immigration Policy, 1850–1990*. Stanford, Calif.: Stanford University Press.

Pastor, M. 1993. *Latinos and the Los Angeles Uprising: The Economic Context*. Claremont, Calif.: Tomás Rivera Center.

Pearlstone, Z. 1989. *Ethnic L.A.* Beverly Hills, Calif.: Hillcrest Press.

Peters, E. D. 1998. Recent structural changes in Mexico's economy: A preliminary analysis of some sources of Mexican migration to the United States. In *Crossings: Mexican Immigration in Interdisciplinary Perspectives*, ed. M. M. Suarez-Orozco. Cambridge, Mass.: Harvard University Press.

Portes, A., and R. Rumbaut. 1996. *Immigrant America: A Portrait*. Berkeley: University of California Press.

Reisler, M. 1976. *By the Sweat of Their Brow: Mexican Immigrant Labor in the United States, 1900–1940.* Westport, Conn.: Greenwood Press.

Report of the Senate Judiciary Committee for the Use of the Select Commission of Immigration and Refugee Policy. 1980. 96th Cong., 2d sess. *History of the Immigration and Naturalization Service.* Washington, D.C.: Government Printing Office.

Rolph, E. 1990. *A Window on Immigration Reform: Implementing IRCA in Los Angeles.* Santa Monica, Calif.: RAND Corporation.

Romzek, B. 1999. Reforming Medicaid through contracting: The nexus of implementation and organizational culture. *Journal of Public Administration* 9: 107–139.

Rourke, F. E., ed. 1986. *Bureaucratic Power in National Policy Making.* Boston: Little, Brown.

Ruiz, V. 1998. *From Out of the Shadows.* New York: Oxford University Press.

Sanchez, G. J. 1993. *Becoming Mexican American.* New York: Oxford University Press.

Sassen, S. 1994. *The Mobility of Labor and Capital.* New York: Cambridge University Press.

Schneider, A., and H. Ingram. Social construction of target populations: Implications for politics and policy. *American Political Science Review* (June): 334–346.

Sears, D. O. 1988. Symbolic racism. In *Eliminating Racism: Profiles in Controversy,* ed. P. A. Katz and D. A. Taylor, 53–84. New York: Plenum Press.

Short, M. and L. Magaña. 2002. Political rhetoric, immigration attitudes and contemporary prejudice: A Mexican American dilemma. *Journal of Social Psychology* 6: 142.

Simon, H., D. Smithburg, and V. Thompson. 1986. The struggle for organizational survival. In *Bureaucratic Power in National Policy Making,* ed. F. E. Rourke, 17–28. Boston: Little, Brown.

Solis, J. 1990. *Los Angeles County Latino Assessment Study.* Claremont, Calif.: Tomás Rivera Center.

Stephan, W. G. 1986. Intergroup relations. In *The Handbook of Social Psychology,* 3d ed., ed. G. Lindzey and E. Aronson, 600–658. New York: Random House.

Trueba, E. T. 1998. The education of Mexican immigrant children. In *Crossings: Mexican Immigration in Interdisciplinary Perspectives,* ed. M. M. Suarez-Orozco, 251–280. Cambridge, Mass.: Harvard University Press.

Tucker, R. 1990. *Immigration and U.S. Foreign Policy.* Boulder, Colo.: Westview Press.

Tomás Rivera Center. 1994. *California School District Administrators Speak to Proposition 187: A TRC Survey.* Claremont, Calif.: Tomás Rivera Center.

U.S. Commission on Immigration Reform. 1997a. *Becoming an American: Immigration and Immigrant Policy.*

———. 1997b. *Becoming an American: Executive Summary.*

U.S. Congress. 1985. *History of the Immigration and Naturalization Service, prepared for the 96th Congress.* Washington, D.C.: Government Printing Office.

———. 1986. Immigration Reform and Control Act of 1986. PL 99–603 S. 1200.

———. 1989. A review of the implementation of the Immigration Reform and Control Act of 1986. *A Report by the Office of Congressman Charles E. Schumer.* March 6.

U.S. Department of Justice. 1989. *Special Audit of the Immigration and Naturalization Service.* February. Prepared by Audit Justice Management Division.

———. 2001. INS *Restructuring Plan: Immigration and Naturalization Service.* Washington, D.C.

U.S. Immigration and Naturalization Service (INS). 1999. *1998 Statistical Yearbook of the Immigration and Naturalization Service.* Springfield, Va.: National Technical Information Service.

Vernez, G. 1989. *Immigration and International Relations: Proceedings of a Conference on the International Effects of 1986 Immigration Reform and Control Act.* Santa Monica, Calif.: RAND Corporation.

Wilson, T. D. 1997. Theoretical approaches to Mexican wage labor migration. In *New American Destinies: A Reader in Contemporary Asian and Latino Immigration,* ed. D. Y. Hamamoto and R. D. Torres, 47–72. New York: Routledge.

Newspaper Articles

Alvord, V. 1998. Mexican consular office set at border; angry agents lodge protests with INS, Justice Department. *Los Angeles Times,* November 10.

Brownstein, R. 1999. Latino clout, improved economy soften GOP stance on immigration. *Los Angeles Times,* July 19.

Gorman, T. 1992. Temecula won't pursue lawsuits against INS. *Los Angeles Times,* August 14.

Lewis, A. 1998. Immigration nightmare continues. *Denver Post,* November 13.

McDonnel, P. J. 1997. Riordan assails citizenship backlog. *Los Angeles Times,* September 18.

———. 1998. Evolution of a logjam. *Los Angeles Times,* October 5.

Ostrow, R. 1990. INS assailed as wasteful, poorly run, failure-prone. *Los Angeles Times,* November 7.

Parker, S. 1990. INS praised in RAND report. *Los Angeles Daily Journal,* November 6.

Ramos, G. 1990. RAND praises INS' amnesty role in L.A. *Los Angeles Times,* November 6.

Reza, H. G. 1999. Girl dies after injection at makeshift clinic. *Los Angeles Times,* February 25.

Schmitt, E. 1997. Immigration procedures are criticized. *New York Times,* April 19.

Shapiro, W. 1998. Immigration agency reform requires influx of leadership. *USA Today,* April 8.

Suro, R., and D. Balz. 1994. Immigration measure shakes up California. *Washington Post,* November 3.

Yzaguirre, R. 1996. Elections mean open season on U.S. Hispanics. *Houston Chronicle,* June 21.

Index